It is my prayer that each of your children will gain strength, confidence, and clarity as he or she celebrates on the pages of this book. May you and your child enjoy the celebration!

Pam Farrel

Here's What People Are Saying About **Celebrate!**

"Fresh, delightful, original, and creative! Pam has given us a whole world of spiritual discovery that we can celebrate with our children and grandchildren. What a gifted resource to enrich and create my own teachable moments with our children's children."

Jill P. Briscoe
Author, *Women Who Changed Their World*; speaker

"What a wonderful gift to celebrate with your children! This hands-on spiritual scrapbook will help you and your child catalog precious memories and pass on the baton of faith to future generations."

Claudia Arp
Co-founder, Marriage Alive; co-author, *Suddenly They're 13*

"Pam Farrel gives a wealth of inspirational and practical ideas on how to celebrate your child's spiritual journey. It is a wonderful way to help your child grow in his or her love for Jesus, and to journal those once-in-a-lifetime significant moments in your child's life. Pam has shown us how to capture them forever. This will definitely be one of the first books I give to my daughters when I become a grandma. What a legacy of faith to pass down."

Fern Nichols
President and founder of Moms In Touch International

Contents

To my children,

Brock, Zach, and Caleb,

and to the women who will become your wives,

and to the children and grandchildren that you will each have some day:

You have been the inspiration for this book.

A godly heritage was started with Dad and me.

It is our prayer that you each pass the baton of faith,

generation to generation.

Let this be written for a future generation,
that a people not yet created may praise the Lord.
Psalm 102:18

Introduction

Attics are wonderful places. They are an eclectic mix of memories and mayhem. They are filled with boxes of half-used crayons and toys tossed aside for the excitement of a new stage of life. And if you are fortunate, somewhere amidst all the remainders of days gone by are reminders of a life well lived, a legacy passed on, words penned with the purpose of encouraging those who would come after this life was gone.

A friend visiting our church shared that while helping her parents reorganize all the treasures and timeworn articles in their attic, she came across her great-grandfather's old Bible. Our friend was the newlywed bride of a missionary, and they were in the process of fundraising, completing the paperwork, and training for the mission field. As she picked up the tattered copy of God's Word that had been painstakingly marked by her great-grandfather, she noted that his prayer requests were written on the flyleaf. One in particular was a prayer for missionaries to be sent to a specific country. Her great-grandfather's heart for that country was poured out in a few short sentences. Her heart beat a little faster as she realized she was to be the answer to her great-grandfather's prayer. The country scrawled in her great-grandfather's well-worn Bible was Japan, and she had just married a Japanese pastor. They were headed back to his homeland to begin the work of sharing God's Good News. Even as she shared the story with me, she was excited. A mantle had been passed, values had been shared, beliefs had been handed from one generation to another.

Passing the baton of faith is the heart of **Celebrate!** My desire for this book came when my oldest son (who at the writing of this book is sixteen) was six. Brock had many spiritual questions as a child, and I'd write his comments in his baby book. Age 3: *Mom, I heard Dad tell about when Jesus is coming back and that He would be riding a white horse.*

Does that mean there are animals in heaven? Age 4: *Mom, if God is good, and Satan is bad, how did that happen? In Sunday School today we learned God created everything and said, "It is good," so how come Satan isn't good?* (You see my oldest had me on my spiritual toes from the beginning!)

Once, while Bill and I were training our youth ministry staff at a family camp, Brock was sad and wanted his mommy and daddy, so the baby-sitter came to retrieve us. It happened to be my turn to do the training, so Bill went and sat with Brock on the cabin steps under the starry sky. Brock was again asking some deep spiritual questions. Bill thought, *Wow! Maybe this is the moment. Maybe Brock wants to make a decision to trust God personally. Maybe Brock wants to begin his journey of making his faith his own.* (Brock was only around three at the time, but Bill, a first-time, over-anxious, over-achieving pastor, thought he better be sure. Even though Brock was young, it was easy for a first-time dad to think maybe his son was a spiritual prodigy!)

Bill asked, "Brock, would you like to invite Jesus into your heart?"

Brock pondered this for a moment and said, "No, Dad, when Jesus gets out of the Bible, then I'll ask Him into my life."

And that has been our goal ever since, to get Jesus out of the Bible and into the reality of the world that makes up our children's lives. We've wanted to share all we know about the God who loves us with our children in a way they could understand. We're always looking for the best way to pass on our spiritual heritage in kid lingo.

A few years later, Brock and his younger brother, Zach, were sitting at the dining-room table. It was Father's Day, 1990. Again, Brock began asking spiritual questions, and now that he was a kindergartner and six he wanted some real answers. Again, Bill sensed that maybe Brock was ready to take the step into his own faith, so that afternoon, Bill and I explained the plan of salvation by grace to our son. In response, Brock prayed and received Christ into his life as his personal Savior. This was a big decision! I wanted to celebrate and commemorate this very important occasion!

I remember wishing I had more details about the things that led up to my own decision to follow Christ. I remembered bits and pieces. I had jotted a memo in the front of the new Bible my mother had given me on my baptismal day. My mother, an avid photographer, had caught a few important snapshots of some important events in my spiritual growth—vacation Bible school programs, my baptism, Christmas programs—but because she too was very young in her faith, didn't think to catalog or journal any remembrances of my spiritual journey. I wanted my children to be able to look back and be able to remember the details of their spiritual journey and have a place that captured their budding faith and our parental feelings about it.

Wanting a way to remember is a common maternal instinct. It's why we take snapshots, place drawings on the refrigerator door, audio and video tape many precious moments in time. Not only do we long to remember ourselves, but we desire our children have these moments in time impressed upon their memories as well. Elisa Morgan, president of Mothers of Preschoolers (MOPS), expressed her thoughts after her own preschool children made decisions to trust Christ for themselves. She writes, "They're so young, will this decision stick? When she's twelve, will she even remember this moment?" I am very familiar with that motivation.

I thought surely there was a resource out there in some Christian bookstore, or at some convention, that would do this—but there wasn't. After looking for a gift to commemorate Brock's big decision, and not finding one, I went home, prayed for creativity, then wrote one! The original *I Made a Big Decision* is in the back of this journal. Every child should have a starting point of faith to celebrate: a conversion, a confirmation, a baptism, a dedication, or a simple prayer of faith. When a child comes to believe in Christ for him or her self, history is changed. The lives of children yet to be born will be different because a legacy of faith will be passed on. My life is radically different because as a child, I

---

1 Elisa Morgan, *Chronicles of Childhood: Recording Your Child's Spiritual Journey* (Grand Rapids, MI: Zondervan, 1996) 11.

came to know that God loved me and wanted a relationship with me. Living out a Christian life was new information in my family tree. I remember feeling so excited about my new relationship with God when I was a child, so excited I used to write little stories about it, so excited I wanted to *Celebrate!* So when my children picked up the baton of faith, I especially wanted to *Celebrate!*

There will be many more reasons to celebrate spiritual growth in the coming years. And, I hope, many more parent/child interactions that will build your child's faith. This journal is filled with those kinds of opportunities.

One way to ensure that your child has a consistent pattern of growth is to complete this journal/scrapbook together. When a child has a journal filled with his or her own legacy, he or she will enter the teen years with confidence. And then as an adult, he or she has a legacy, a written heritage, to pass on to his or her own children and grandchildren. *Celebrate!* is an heirloom scribbled in kid-print. *Celebrate!* is an opportunity to party with a purpose! It is designed so that year after year the child can celebrate his or her growth in God. Here is a built-in opportunity to celebrate your child's spiritual birthday year after year. You and your child can choose the initial celebration, special event, or decision to commemorate. Then each year, around that date, pull out the journal and encourage your son or daughter to complete the fun activities. Add in your reflections (you can also use the journal all year as your child says funny or profound things, does spiritually significant things, or when you want to record a spiritually significant moment). Each chapter contains ideas to help your child grow in his or her faith, skills and truths taught in kid lingo, advice from respected Christian leaders, and fun ideas for spiritual birthday celebrations. Here's a sneak preview of what you'll find in each chapter:

Memory Makers: (Advice from parents who've been there.)

Kid Quotes! (Funny quotes about God.)

My Quotes! (You can record your child's profound or comical statements here.)

It's a Party! Kid Celebrations of Faith (For-kids-only activities to help them learn skills and truths to grow in their own walk with God.)

Happy Spiritual Birthday to You! (Ideas to make these annual celebrations something to look forward to.)

Reflections (Mom, Dad, or both, grandparents, or aunts and uncles can record their personal thoughts about the child's spiritual growth the past year.) You can make simple notes of remembering special days or conversations. You can do it in the form of a letter to your child complimenting the growth of the past year. You can also try something creative: make a photo collage with subtitles, a newsletter with a front-page headline look, a feature article written about your child, or a flier with lots of graphics that highlights the important moments of the year. However you choose to format it, make it a personal cheering section for growth you've seen and hopes and dreams for the future.

Dear God: (The child will get to write a letter to God about his or her relationship with Him the past year.) Plenty of sentence starters are given so even the nonwriter can create a remembrance. Early on, you might help your child by playing secretary if he or she hasn't learned to write yet. But by first grade or so most children can create their own note to their Heavenly Father.

Dear God and **It's a Party! Kid Celebrations of Faith** will all be bordered with footprints or handprints so the children can spot them. Each chapter also contains some unique spiritual insights to help your child grow in his or her spiritual development in the coming year. There are pages to tape or glue in drawings, Sunday School papers, important documents and certificates, and pocket pages for cards and other hard-to-paste items. Feel free to include photos or any other remembrances in each chapter. If you have a very artistic child, and your fridge is covered with magnificent drawings, to save space you can make color copies (shrunk down in size), save the smaller copies, and place them in the journal. (My youngest son could fill numerous journals just with his drawings so we've found this trick works well!) There are several pages at the end that you can use for extra papers, artwork, or for your reflections in the years following the journal.

Invest in some colored pencils and markers, stickers, or anything else you think would help your child enjoy this journal. And enjoy it they will. My sons look forward to anytime we write something in their journals. Often, after they have said something funny or significant, they ask, "Are we going to write that down?" My oldest two sons have used their journals to write their personal testimonies. Because they have the details of their spiritual growth recorded, preparing their story to be shared publicly was a much easier task.

When my oldest, Brock, was a freshman in high school, he prepared his personal story into a three-minute talk to give to a team meeting/pizza party for his football team. Out of the sixty-eight who were invited, forty-five came, and after Brock shared his personal story, twenty-six prayed and began a new relationship with God. Each season, Brock, who was the team captain for three different sports his freshman year, held parties where he shared his story. At the end of his freshman year, thirty-six of his friends had made decisions to begin a relationship with God because of those parties. As a sophomore, he has launched a Fellowship of Christian Athletes club on his campus and it is continuing to grow.

Brock credits his focus and confidence to several sources, including his involvement in great groups like Student Venture, Fellowship of Christian Athletes, and Teen Extreme youth group at church. But his greatest confidence is credited to those quieter days when faith was passed from dad to son, from mother to son and then recorded. Brock can look back on his growth and gain the assurance that God has been with him, step by step, that God has prepared him, all along the way, and that the future is bright because God "will never leave or forsake" him.

Kid Celebrations of Faith

Happy Spiritual Birthday to me! My parents are so excited because

[Mom/Dad, fill in the decision/event.] _____

_____

I am very happy. Here is a picture of me smiling (photo or drawing):

God is happy too. God says I am a member of His family (John 1:12). When I look around at the beautiful world God created, I can see God's happiness. The bright sunny sky, the beautiful flowers, the chirping birds, and rainbows after the storm all show God's love. (On the next page, draw a picture of a rainbow, some beautiful flowers, birds, or the sunny sky.)

In the Bible, a wise man named John said, "I have no greater joy than to hear that my children are walking in the truth" (3 John 4). John was a follower of Jesus. It makes Jesus happy when you know and follow the truth. The truth is:

God loves me.

I need God to love me.

I love God.

Because I love God, I want to learn what He says in the Bible and I want to do it.

When I obey God it makes His heart happy.

In the hearts below, draw some things you do that make God's heart happy. Things like helping your friends or mom or dad. Maybe being nice to your sister or brother or a pet.

Reading the Bible also makes God happy. (Or if you can't read yet, God loves it when the Bible is read to you!) What is your favorite place in your house? God likes to know our favorite things. He likes to share favorite places together. Draw a picture of you in your favorite place reading the Bible.

The Bible is God's love letter to people. God loves for you to read His letter often. What time of the day would you like to read the Bible? (In the morning, at lunch, at bedtime, at naptime?)

I would like to read the Bible at_____.

In this book, there will be times that you will be asked to look up verses from the Bible. This is how you can find the verse. For example: **John 3:16.**

John is the book. **3** is the chapter. **16** is the verse.

Now look up John 3:16 in the Bible. What does it say? Write it here:

_____

_____

_____

_____

_____

_____

_____

Now write a letter to God.

[Mom/Dad, if your child doesn't write yet or gets overwhelmed at the length of the writing, have him or her dictate the letter to you and you write it. Remember to date this letter.]

Tell God about your exciting decision. Tell Him about your special day. Tell Him some of your favorite things (favorite foods, toys, friends, or games, for example). Thank God for as many things as you can think of. Thank God for loving you.

_____

_____

_____

_____

_____

_____

Memory Makers

Advice from Parents Who've Been There

FRAME THE MOMENT!

In our home, when I was expecting, we chose our child's names (one if it was a boy, another if a girl). Then after we knew the sex of the child, we looked up the meaning of the selected name and chose a verse that reflected the name and had a plaque created that included the name, the meaning, the spiritual meaning, and the verse. These hang outside our children's bedrooms so our children know what our hopes and dreams are for them as they grow. This is what hangs outside our sons' bedrooms:

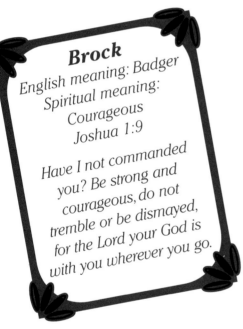

Brock
English meaning: Badger
Spiritual meaning:
Courageous
Joshua 1:9

Have I not commanded you? Be strong and courageous, do not tremble or be dismayed, for the Lord your God is with you wherever you go.

Zachery
Spiritual meaning:
The Lord has remembered
Jeremiah 15:15-16

Thou who knowest, O Lord, remember me, take notice of me, and take vengeance for me on my persecutors. Do not, in view of Thy patience take me away; know that for Thy sake I endure reproach. Thy words were found and I ate them, and they became for me, a joy and the delight of my heart; for I have been called by Thy name, O Lord God of hosts.

Caleb Joshua
Caleb: Brave One
Joshua: Hebrew for Jesus
Numbers 14:24

My servant Caleb, because he has a different spirit and has followed me fully.

Memory Makers cont'd

KiD QUoteS!

"My daughter, Laura, went with me to buy some grape juice for our church's Communion service. Telling her it was for the Lord's Supper, I put it in the refrigerator. Later, her older brother, Jonathan, saw it and wanted some. Laura scolded, 'No, that's for God's lunch!'"
— *Melanie Bell, Texas*[2]

MY QUoteS!

_____

_____

_____

_____

_____

_____

_____

_____

_____

_____

1. 1 Timothy 4:12.
2. *Today's Christian Woman*, January/February 1996, 25.

Whenever I see the traits of the boys' names displayed in something they say or do, I will point it out to them and compliment them. For example, when Caleb, our Mr. Precise, wants to make sure everyone follows the rules to the letter, I say, "Wow, Caleb, your name says that you will follow God fully. Integrity is important to you, isn't it? You want people to follow the laws and rules, don't you?"

Or a few days ago when Brock was asked to open up the city council in prayer and he confidently said: "Hello, my name is Brock Farrel. I am the JV quarterback for San Marcos High School and the president of the Fellowship of Christian Athletes Club on campus. You have met my parents, Pam and Bill Farrel, because they have both been asked to open these meetings in prayer also. On behalf of all the youth of our community, I want to thank you for leading us. Shall we pray? 'Dear Lord, We thank You for our leaders, and we pray that You would give them wisdom tonight. We also pray for the youth of our city. I pray that these verses from the Bible would be true of all of us who are young: *Don't let anyone look down on you because you are young, but set an example for the believers in speech, in life, in love, in faith and in purity.*[1] God, help us all, young and mature, look to You as our hope and salvation. Amen.'"

Afterward, I complimented him on his composure, his choice to wear a suit and tie, his confidence and reminded him of his journey to courage. As a young boy, he was small, and he would get tussled about in play by older kids; I reminded him that God helped him learn not to whine, but to be courageous in small and big situations. I recalled to him that he was afraid at first to share his faith with his friends, but because he's courageously done it over and over, now he was given a platform to share his faith with adults as well.

He just smiled and said, "Yeah, it is pretty cool how God works. But Mom, I've been raised to think courageously so doesn't it seem natural that I would act courageously?"

I smiled, knowing it all started the week he was born and I hung that little sign outside his door.

Happy Spiritual Birthday to You!

Since this year marks the first spiritual birthday celebration, host a party for your child with all the birthday trappings: cake, candle (one), and—if you'd like—balloons, streamers, and a few friends. Feel free to reword the happy birthday song to say "Happy spiritual birthday to you …" Sure that might tweak the tune a bit, but it will be fun all the same. Or insert a favorite Sunday School song like "Jesus Loves the Little Children."

Choose to give gifts each year on the anniversary of this date, gifts to help the child grow spiritually. Bible storybooks, audio and videotapes, journals, devotionals, Bible games, and music tapes are just a few ideas to try.

If your church or beliefs encouraged you to choose godparents for your child, invite them to celebrate with you. Even if your church doesn't have a formal ceremony for the choosing of godparents, you can still ask specific people to make the commitment to contribute to your child's spiritual development throughout his or her life. Spiritually successful children are surrounded by many adults who reinforce spiritual principles and live as godly role models and available sounding boards for the developing child.

Angel Party!

The heavens celebrate our human decisions to follow Jesus. We have chosen to follow God's example and we look for ways to celebrate. One of the ways our family celebrates is by hosting Angel Parties. We first began Angel Parties when our children made decisions for Christ. And now we also have Angel Parties to celebrate when anyone in our family introduces someone to Jesus. Early on I had the boys cut out angel pictures, and added angel stickers and stamps so they each could make a personal angel place mat for the celebrations. We laminated the works of art. We would eat angel food cake, talk about the special moment that was being celebrated, and we'd relive it in conversation.

As the boys have gotten older, they've outgrown the cute place mats, and none of them really love angel food cake, so we have the person in charge of the celebration choose the food or the place to eat out and the celebration continues in a more grown-up form. The style of the angel party may evolve over the years, but the principle of celebration is seared into our children's minds. Each child in our family knows: It is important that people know God and knowing God is reason to celebrate!

REFLECTIONS

A child's life is full of exciting beginnings: those first few wobbling steps, learning the A, B, Cs, the day he or she can manage the crayon long enough to scrawl out the letters of his or her name. Beginnings, we all love to celebrate them. We call our spouse at the office with a "Guess what Johnny just did!" or we brag to our neighbors or grandparents as we beam with pride over the newest accomplishment of our "exceptional" child. Spiritual beginnings are equally, if not more, exciting because a child's entire future is shaped by his or her spiritual beliefs. The spiritual development of your children creates the blueprint for their lives.

Depending on your church, a variety of events can create the foundation of faith. A decision for Christ, a confirmation ceremony, or a public dedication of faith that reflects a private decision to believe in God and follow Him can all mark the moment when a child steps into his or her own faith. When children are small, dress-up is a normal activity. Your daughter might prance around in your high heels and your son clomps through the kitchen in your boots. Those days make us smile. But nothing can compare to the joy of knowing that our children have decided that faith isn't just for Mom and Dad but for them as well.

Foundations are laid by these first steps of faith. These precious early moments should be marked in time and engraved into a child's memory. We painstakingly send off the set of white infant shoes and have them bronzed to tangibly mark our child's first steps, but few families permanently mark significant spiritual moments with such care.

In the introduction, I explained my desperate search for some significant way to mark and commemorate the first big decision of faith my son made. (If you'd like your child to complete all or part of that original book, *I Made A Big Decision*, it is on page 96). I sat down with each of my children after he had made this decision for Christ and explained the concept of a spiritual birthday.

Marking a spiritual beginning isn't a new concept. God threw the first party. The angels in heaven rejoice when a sinner decides to turn to God. Heaven celebrates the decision (Luke 15:10). The Bible says when anyone is in Christ they are new! (2 Cor. 5:17) When a house foundation is poured and sidewalks are laid with cement, a family often marks the new house by placing hand and footprints in the hardening cement with the date. It is a marker of a new start. Families should mark spiritual beginnings with the same joy and care. I wanted to celebrate when each of my children launched out on his own spiritual journey. I gave a personal gift—much like a birthday present. Since my children were just learning to read and write, I gave them a video from the Christian bookstore and, in permanent marker, I wrote the occasion and date so each time the children would watch it they would remember how and why that particular video came into our home. I recorded the date and decision in the family Bible, and we completed *I Made a Big Decision.* Each son, when we got to the end of the small book, said something to the effect of: "Mom, that was cool. Is there more?" And that was the beginning of my trying to create more ways to celebrate.

You may want to also include, in this first reflection letter, some very early "firsts." When did you first pray for your child? When did you first pray over your child? When did you first pray with your child? When did he or she attend church the first time? What was his or her first spiritual word or conversation with you? Brock's first spiritual word was *Bible.* He started with all the *B* words first—book, ball, Bible. Try to summarize how you felt when these firsts happened. If you don't remember them or didn't record them, that's okay, just start from this moment and go forward commemorating and celebrating your child's growth in God.

YOUR REFLECTION

Each chapter, each year, you will be asked to reflect on your child's development, or gather reflections from others in your child's life. This year, write out your feelings about your child's decision, the spiritually significant event, or the foundation that has been laid. You can interview friends and family about their feelings and impressions and include them too. You might decide to reflect on your own faith walk as well and add remembrances from your childhood. Celebrate your child's faith on the following page.

We will not hide them from their children;
we will tell the next generation
the praiseworthy deeds of the Lord,
his power, and the wonders he has done.
Psalm 78:4

REFLECTIONS cont'd

Dear God

Okay kids! Here's your chance to write a letter to God. Write out your prayer requests for the coming year, and finish the sentences below. Let God know what's on your heart. He loves and cares about you!

God, first off, I'd like to thank You for
_____

_____

_____

_____

So far, the highlights of this year have been
_____

_____

God, this year I'd like for You to take care of
_____

_____

I'd like it if You would please give me
_____

_____

And if You would please give my mom
_____

_____

my dad

_____

- -

_____

and my family

_____

- -

_____

I would really appreciate it. But only if You think these things will be good for us.

I also have some other people who are very special to me. Please bless:

_____

- -

_____

Dear God, one last thing, could You please

_____

- -

_____

Thank You very much, God. I love You. Amen.
Sincerely,

_____

Remember, God is celebrating your decision to believe in Him and His love for you!

Kid Celebrations of Faith

Having a relationship with Jesus is like having a best friend. Only Jesus is a very special friend. Like a best friend, He loves us and shares all His favorite things with us. For example: Because Jesus loves you, He forgave all your sin. Sin is the bad things we say and do. Sin just means we are NOT perfect. But Jesus is perfect. That's why He died on the cross for us. His perfection paid the price for our imperfection.

Let's compare Jesus' love to how your brother (if you have one) might love you. Let's say you did something really bad, like throw something in the house and it broke a window. Your parents punish you and tell you that you will have to work for five days all day long at your uncle's store to earn the money to replace the window. Your brother, who wasn't even home when you broke the window, realizes that you will have to miss playing in your first football game (or girls, miss your ballet recital) because you have to work in the store. Your brother volunteers to take your punishment, not just on the football game day—but all five days. That's sacrificial love—it's kind of like what Jesus did for you—but Jesus' gift was hundreds and thousands times better and more important!

There are so many good things about having Jesus as a best friend. Here are a few:

If we sin (do something wrong), He forgives us if we confess (tell the truth about what we did). (You can find this in God's Word, 1 John 1:9.) How do you feel when you've done something wrong and then you are forgiven? Draw a picture of how you feel when you are forgiven:

John 15:7 says, "If you remain in me and my words remain in you, ask whatever you wish, and it will be given you." Jesus wants us to abide (stay) close to Him and share our heart with Him. Draw something you prayed about this year that Jesus answered.

Jesus says He will be with us always (Matt. 28:20). He will be with you in elementary school, He will be with you in high school and college, and He will be with you when you start your job and get married and

24

when you have children of your own. Why don't you draw a picture of these things? And as you draw a picture of each of these seasons of your life, thank Jesus that He will always be with you.

You in elementary school

You in middle school or high school

You at your first job

You driving your first car

You in college, or getting married

You when you are a mom or dad with your own children

Someday, we will live in heaven with Jesus. Heaven is a place where there are no tears, where the streets are made of gold, and Jesus' glory will light up heaven brighter than the sun! (The glory of Jesus is His "shininess" from being the Creator, and most powerful, strongest, most amazing awesome God! Wow!) Draw a picture of what you think heaven will look like: [Mom/Dad, for some clues read Rev. 21:10-27.]

Jesus is a best friend. Who are your other friends? Draw a picture of you and one or two of your friends.

KID QUOTES!

"My three-year-old cousin, Mark, accidentally spilled his fruit punch on the floor one day. He decided to clean up the mess himself and dashed to the back porch to get the mop. Suddenly realizing it was dark outside, he became apprehensive about reaching out the door for the mop. His mother reminded him that Jesus was everywhere—even in the dark. Mark thought for a minute. Then, putting his face to the door he said, 'Jesus, if You are out there, will You hand me the mop?'"

—*Kathy Martin, Tennessee.*[1]

MY QUOTES!

_____

_____

_____

_____

_____

_____

_____

_____

_____

_____

1. *Today's Christian Woman*, January/February 1996, 25.

Memory Makers
Advice from Parents Who've Been There

Dr. James Dobson is a household name in the area of child rearing. His daily radio broadcast, *Focus on the Family*, is heard by millions around the world. However, his children didn't grow up waiting to hear the broadcast each day. No, his kids, Ryan and Danae, looked forward to carpool days when Dad drove and told them "Woof" stories. Woof was a fictional dog whose high jinks and adventures brought biblical truths home to his children's hearts as they rode in the car.

Woof was a heroic dog, with a floppy ear, crooked leg, and a bent tail, but he captured the heart of Danae. When she was twelve years old she wrote and published her first *Woof* book; now there is a *Woof* series, so the storytelling legacy continues.

Seems like Jim Dobson isn't the only dad who likes storytelling to communicate spiritual truths. Many of today's favorite Christian children's books came about the same way. John Trent, a counselor and president of Encouraging Words, captures biblical principles in *I'd Choose You, There's a Duck in my Closet,* and *The Spider Sisters.* Chuck Swindoll, for years a storytelling senior pastor of one of America's largest churches and the voice heard on the *Insight for Living* radio broadcast, now tells stories to his grandchildren, and they have been published in *Paw Paw Chuck's Big Ideas in the Bible.* Max Lucado, a pastor and father, warms the heart of his own children, and now others, with *The Crippled Lamb* and other books for children.

Why don't you try your hand at storytelling? Read one of these books with your child for inspiration. Launch your own storytelling with true stories from your childhood that taught you a lesson, then venture off into fiction and create some memorable tales of your own. As I write, *VeggieTales* videos are at the top of the market. Who would have thought cucumbers and tomatoes would have ever captured the imaginations of children? It's the power of the story. As you tuck your children in bed tonight, tell a story.

Happy Spiritual Birthday to You!

As a way to mark the growth in your child's life, you may want to create a tangible remembrance. The Book of Joshua tells a story of the nation of Israel crossing the Jordan into the Promised Land. When the priests stepped into the water, the river dried up, even though it was at flood stage. As a remembrance of all God had done, God told them:

> "Choose twelve men from among the people, one from each tribe, and tell them to take up twelve stones from the middle of the Jordan from right where the priests stood and to carry them over with you and put them down at the place where you stay tonight."

> So Joshua called together the twelve men … and said to them, "Go over before the ark of the Lord your God into the middle of the Jordan. Each of you is to take up a stone on his shoulder, according to the number of the tribes of the Israelites, to serve as a sign among you. In the future, when your children ask you, 'What do these stones mean?' tell them that the flow of the Jordan was cut off before the ark of the covenant of the Lord. When it crossed the Jordan, the waters of the Jordan were cut off. These stones are to be a memorial to the people of Israel forever."

> So the Israelites did as Joshua commanded them. … And Joshua set up at Gilgal the twelve stones they had taken out of the Jordan. He said to the Israelites, "In the future when your descendants ask their fathers, 'What do these stones mean?' tell them, 'Israel crossed the Jordan on dry ground.' For the Lord your God dried up the Jordan before you until you had crossed over. The Lord your God did to the Jordan just what he had done to the Red Sea when he dried it up before us until we had crossed over. He did this so that all the peoples of the earth might know that the hand of the Lord is powerful and so that you might always fear the Lord your God."
> (Josh. 4:2-8 and 20-24. The full story is in Joshua 3:15–4:24.)

In the same way, your child needs visual reminders that God is working in his or her life and that He is aware of growth physically, socially, emotionally, and spiritually. A few ideas for ways to create a tangible reminder: plant a tree and take a picture of your child in front of the tree each year on his or her spiritual birthday. Read verses from Psalm 1 as a reminder that a life rooted in a relationship with God is a strong life.

Make a memory stone. Pour a small block of cement, like a stepping-stone, etch in your child's spiritual birthday, and add a favorite verse or highlight from the past year. You may want to do this in symbolic form: the ocean or sunset for baptism; a heart for leading a friend to Christ; a rainbow for God answering a big prayer request and showing He keeps

His promises. Create a path with your child's stepping-stones in a garden. (You can add them year after year, or each member of your family can create a stone for the year you create a garden path.) Include the child in planting the garden and talk about growth in Christ.

Donate a piece of equipment, or some other tangible gift, to a place that consistently helps your child grow: a preschool or school, a camp, or your church. Include your child in the decision of what to give each year. Talk about the need to freely give just as we have freely received.

By creating a tangible marker, year after year, a visible legacy is formed. The visible legacy can become a place of comfort later if hard times or emotionally rocky circumstances hit your child's life in the teen or adult years.

REFLECTIONS

This is a great place to share some of the answers to things you've prayed for your child over the past year. Add other answers to prayer you've had this year, especially as they relate to your family.

_____

_____

_____

_____

_____

_____

_____

_____

_____

_____

_____

_____

_____

_____

_____

Developing a Prayer Plan

Fern Nichols, founder of Moms in Touch, an international prayer ministry, encourages her own children to lift all their requests to God. "Nothing is too trivial to pray about," says Fern. "If it's a worry to them, then it's okay to pray about." Fern uses a fourfold prayer plan similar to ACTS as a pattern for her own children. In addition, some of her hints to help develop a child's prayer life include:

✔ Pray every night together. Ask your child, "How can I pray for you?"

✔ Try praying just one subject each night, but pray for that area thoroughly. For example, pray for all his or her teachers or friends or family. Praying this way helps encourage a child to dialogue with God.

✔ Use prayer to calm fears. One of Fern's sons suffered from terrible night fears when he was small. Together they memorized verses to help combat fear: 1 John 4:18, Isa. 41:10, Psalm 4:8. The fears disappeared, and to this day the verses come to his mind when he hits any circumstance that might be causing anxiety.

✔ Allow them to be free to pray any way they feel comfortable. Once, one of the Nichols children got up and pointed to each food as he thanked God for it as the family sat down for dinner.

✔ Create a photo album of answers to prayer the child has experienced. Fern created a photo album complete with verses that coincided with special events in that child's life from birth to eighteen. The album was the first item each child packed as he or she went off to college. The scrapbook became a great tool for the grown children to use to share Jesus with their new college friends.

✔ If a child hits a stage where he or she doesn't want to pray with Mom and Dad, then simply say, "That's okay, just let me pray a blessing on you before you sleep" (or leave for school, or an event, and so on). As her sons got older, Fern would often just pass one of her sons, give him a big hug, and pray aloud, "Lord, bless this son I love so much!" Then she'd walk away, leaving a smiling son behind her.

More than anything else, Fern advises modeling prayer and relaying God's Word to the child in all kinds of everyday circumstances. "How can a child trust a God he or she doesn't know?" Nichols encourages, "Decide ahead of time to be disciplined and delight yourself in the Lord in your own prayer life. Then your children will see that God is always there for them."[2]

---

2. Personal interview with Fern Nichols, January 5, 1999. Moms in Touch, PO Box 1120, Poway, CA 92074-1120; 800-949-moms.

Dear God

Okay, now it's your turn to write a letter to your best friend! A great way to talk to God is using the acrostic ACTS:

A is for adore. Tell God how great He is. (He already knows, but He knows it is good for us to say it and remember it!)

Now try writing your own song or poem to God. It doesn't have to be fancy. You could just write out Jesus' name and choose words to describe Jesus: There's even a list of words on the side to choose from! For example:

J (just)

E (excellent, exciting, extremely good)

S (superb, super, Savior)

U (unique, unlike any other, under no one!)

S (satisfying, sure, steady)

[Parents: If your child is older, or up for a challenge, try this exercise with every letter from the alphabet and see if together you can think of a trait of God, a description of Jesus for each letter! This is how Psalm 119 is constructed—but using the Hebrew alphabet.]

C in ACTS is for confess. That just means to tell God anything you know you've done wrong. (He already knows it, but it is good for us to own up to it and tell Him anyway!)

Can you think of anything wrong you have done, said, or thought lately? You can write an "I'm sorry" note here:

_____

_____

_____

_____

T in ACTS is for thanksgiving. Now thank God for some of the especially good things, favorite memories, best things about your home, family, or church. It's good to have a thankful heart.

S in ACTS is for supplication. It's just a big word for "shopping list." When you go to the store, your mom has a list of things you need and want. God wants us to pray and ask Him for things we need or want or things people we know need or want. Be careful here, God wants to give us things that are good for us. If He doesn't think it is good for us, He will say no. He says yes to things in His plan for us, things that will be good for us (James 1:17). Write a list of things and people you would like to pray for in the next year. The sentence starters below will help you remember everyone.

Dear God,
Please help Mom
And help Dad
Please help my cousins and aunts and uncles too. Here's a list and a request I am praying for each of them.

_____

_____

_____

_____

Help my grandma(s) and grandpa(s) to

_____

- -

_____

I have some special teachers I want to pray for too. They are: (list their names and what you are praying for.)

_____

- -

_____

_____

- -

_____

And finally, God, could You help me

_____

- -

_____

And one more time, I'd like to thank You for

_____

- -

_____

Amen

Then we your people, the sheep of your pasture,

will praise you forever;

from generation to generation

we will recount your praise.

Psalm 79:13

Kid Celebrations of Faith

Do you know what your name means? My name means _____
_____

Ask your mom and dad to tell you how you were named and write the story here:

God has many names and those names reveal His character. For example: *Jehovah Jireh* means *The Lord will provide*. That means God will take good care of you. Draw a picture of people who take care of you (Maybe your parents, doctor, nurse, or teachers). God takes care of you like those people—even better! He probably uses those people to help care for you too.

Jehovah nissi means *The Lord is my banner.* In past days when the army of Israel went to battle, they placed banner carriers on horses and they rode in first as a sign of victory because God was leading them to conquer. In the heart, draw some pictures of symbols of victory: goalposts, a gold medal, a winner's wreath, a scoreboard, for example. Knowing God is the best decision you will ever make. God makes people winners. God helps people make wise choices. God brings victory to our hearts!

Jehovah Shalom means *The Lord is my peace.* What is the most peaceful place you know of? Draw it:

It feels so good to be in peaceful places. It feels great getting a hug from someone you love. It feels good to be tucked into bed with your favorite toys and blankets. It feels so good to sit in the shade of the tree or hang your feet in a cool brook. Knowing God is better than all those places!

Jehovah raah means *The Lord is your shepherd.* A shepherd takes very good care of little lambs. Shepherds feed their sheep, lead them to water, take care of them if they get hurt, and stand guard at night to protect them. You are God's little lamb. Draw a picture of a lamb.

In the Book of Psalms, there are words to songs that people sang in worship to God. They are like poems of praise. Many of these songs talk about who God is.

They use word pictures, like symbols, that help us remember who God is. A symbol is something that stands for something else. For example, when you see a red sign in this shape you do what?

That's right, you stop because it is a stop sign. The sign is a symbol that helps you remember. Read the verses below and see if you can pick out the word pictures of who God is. Above the word, draw a picture of the symbol. The first one is done for you.

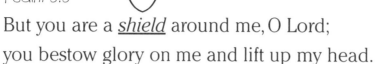

Psalm 3:3

But you are a *shield* around me, O Lord;
you bestow glory on me and lift up my head.

Psalm 18:2

The Lord is my rock, my fortress and my deliverer;
my God is my rock, in whom I take refuge.
He is my shield and the horn of my salvation, my stronghold.

God is a shield, a protector. What are you afraid of? Is it the dark, bullies, lightning storms, or something else that sends chills up your spine?_____
Jesus is your protector. He has many names too. A few of them are: Lion of Judah, Rose of Sharon, King of Kings, Lamb of God. On the shield, draw a picture of your favorite name of Jesus, your shield.

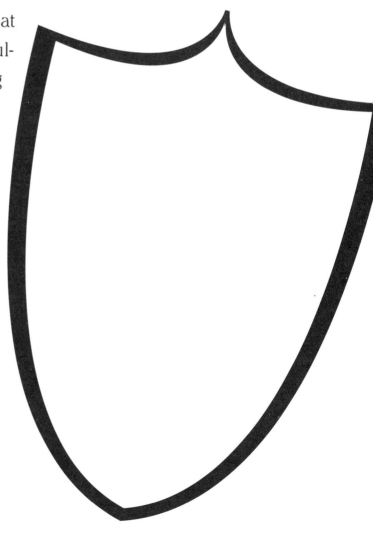

Now read the following verses from psalms and underline all the words like protector, deliverer, and shield. Read the verses again after you have marked them. What are some of the good things about having God be your helper? (For example: Psalm 28:7 says, "The Lord is my strength and my <u>shield</u>;" and the result is :"<u>My heart trusts in him, and I am helped</u>." And the best part is :"<u>My heart leaps for joy</u>." Isn't it great that God is always there to help us? At the right, list the benefits of God's help:

Psalm 7:10

My shield is God Most High,

who saves the upright in heart.

Benefits

Psalm 28:7

The Lord is my strength and my shield;

my heart trusts in him, and I am helped.

My heart leaps for joy

and I will give thanks to him in song.

Psalm 84:11

For the Lord God is a sun and shield;

the Lord bestows favor and honor;

no good thing does he withhold

from those whose walk is blameless.

Psalm 119:114

You are my refuge and my shield;

I have put my hope in your word.

Psalm 144:2

He is my loving God and my fortress,

my stronghold and my deliverer,

my shield, in whom I take refuge,

who subdues peoples under me.

We don't ever need to be afraid. When you are afraid, just talk to God about it and thank God for being your shield. Picture the very strongest person in the whole world that you can think of. Now draw a picture of that person.

Isn't it great? God is even stronger than that!
Turn your ear to me, come quickly to my rescue;
be my rock of refuge, a strong fortress to save me.
Since you are my rock and my fortress,
for the sake of your name lead and guide me (Psalm 31:2-3).

The Bible says God is like a fort. God is like a super strong castle made of stone. The psalmist writes, "God is my bulwark." That is a tall tower at the corners of a fortified city, fort, or castle. These towers were so high that from the top you could see your enemies. The tower had windows made so your enemy's arrows could not come inside, but you could shoot your arrows out through special slits. God has the ability to make us feel just as safe as if we were in the biggest, strongest castle. Draw the biggest, strongest castle you can think of here.

Memory Makers

"Have I not commanded you? Be strong and courageous. Do not be terrified; do not be discouraged, for the Lord your God will be with you wherever you go" (Josh. 1:9).

ZAC'S COURAGE ROCK
"A memorial stone"

To my ten-year-old grandson, Zac, it must have seemed like just another ordinary carpool that day. He was sitting in the front seat, chatting away with friends when, suddenly, the driver of the car passed out at the wheel! The car was traveling sixty-five miles per hour and was locked into cruise control in the fast lane. Quick-thinking Zac grabbed the steering wheel and brought the car to safety on the shoulder of the road. This was not an ordinary day at all, but an extraordinary picture to Zac of God's amazing protection.

As grandparents, we started Zac's rock collection when he was around three years old. It was a way to build memorials, talk about God's Creation, and describe to him what heaven is like. Because I am a Bible study leader, I had discovered there are close to 250 Scriptures that use the words *remember* or *remembrance*, and many of them have to do with remembering the Lord's mighty works. When I heard the story of Zac's courage, I knew this was a moment God would want Zac to remember! The word remember means to *imprint*, a great word to describe what we wanted to see happen in Zac's heart regarding this miracle. So many of the Scriptures on remembering were also linked to having one generation pass on the mighty deeds God had done to the next generation. I thought this moment would be a perfect opportunity to carry out the heart of those passages of Scripture.

We gathered the heads of our family around Zac and read and explained what we saw as God's teaching from the story in Joshua 4. In Joshua 4:6, an explanation of remembrance stones is given: "To serve as a sign among you. In the future, when your children ask you, 'What do these stones mean?'" We wanted this story of Zac's courage and God's protection to be a part of our family's legacy, passed from one generation to another.

We seized the opportunity to add a spiritual rock to Zac's collection. A rock with *courage* etched on it was presented to him with the heads of our family praying: "Lord, may Zac never forget Your keeping power that day on the freeway, may he remember that *courage* comes from You and that You will give it to him to meet the challenges in his life.

Lord, imprint *courage* on his heart by Your mighty hand. Amen."

In the Bible, there are stories of stone monuments erected to remember great acts of God, and even in our culture today, monuments are raised to help us remember great acts of courage. However, God works in the lives of each individual so we all have opportunities to have stones of remembrance. Stone upon stone a child's faith is built. In our family, generations from now, when someone picks up a stone imprinted with *courage* a legacy of God's faithfulness will in turn build another child's faith.

Barbara Christiansen
Escondido, CA

REFLECTIONS

Hear, O Israel: The Lord our God, the Lord is one. Love the Lord your God with all your heart and with all your soul and with all your strength. These commandments that I give you today are to be upon your hearts. Impress them on your children. Talk about them when you sit at home and when you walk along the road, when you lie down and when you get up. Tie them as symbols on your hands and bind them on your foreheads. Write them on the doorframes of your houses and on your gates (Deut. 6:4-9).

In the Old Testament, passing the baton of faith was a big deal. The leaders of Israel took the task seriously. You may have Jewish friends whose children have celebrated a Bar or Bat Mitzvah. According to *The New Manners and Customs of Bible Times*, "The Jewish boy was recognized as entering manhood at thirteen years of age, but it is not certain when this practice began."[1]

When Jewish children are twelve years old, they focus on becoming adults. To prepare for this role, they study very hard. We see the diligence of God in the instructions of Deuteronomy 6:4-9. He wanted the passing of His Word to be preeminent in a family. Parents were to look for opportunities to talk with their children about God and His Word, as they walked, worked, relaxed—always looking for opportunities. It is noted that they were to *"tie them as symbols on your hands and bind them on your foreheads."* This was called a phylactery. It was a small box which contained the familiar first line of this verse: *Hear, O Israel: The Lord our God, the Lord is one. Love the Lord your God with all your heart*

---

1. Ralph Gower, *The New Manners and Customs of Bible Times,* (Chicago: Moody Press, 1987), 63.

and with all your soul and with all your strength. The phylacteries were tied to the wrists and often even to the forehead to remind the Israelites to remember the Lord their God and worship Him alone.

How will you pass on your faith? In this entry reflect on the accomplishments of the past year and growth in your child. Look for significant spiritual moments to celebrate. Look for seeds of faith to applaud and signposts of a possible future calling on his or her life. Brainstorm ways you can place reminders of God in your child's life daily (as you walk, sit, work, on their clothing, on the walls of your home, and so on.) Write out a plan that will help the child celebrate God in his or her life. *Prepare* to celebrate.

When my eldest graduated from eighth grade, one skill we wanted to make sure he had down was the ability to verbally share his faith. We also wanted this passage from middle school to high school to be a big deal—a celebration where he would realize all God had built into his life, his stewardship over those blessings, and a change in the way we, his parents, perceived him as a young man, not a little boy. His graduation party was a sports night held at our local gym and seventy people came, old and young. At the event he shared his personal testimony of faith that he had prepared and publicly thanked those who had built into his life. We recorded the moment on video and in his scrapbook as a marker into adulthood.

KiD QUOteS!

"Preparing my five-year-old son, Keegan, for his first overnight sleepover, I explained, 'Eat whatever is served, say thanks, and make sure you behave yourself.' 'Oh, don't worry, Mom,' Keegan replied, 'I don't sin at anyone else's house.'"

—*Suzy Ryan, California* [2]

MY QUOteS!

2. *Today's Christian Woman*, January/February 1997, 25.

Happy Spiritual Birthday to You!

This year, help your child make something permanent to celebrate his or her faith. Create a webpage or screen saver to commemorate a spiritually significant event, have the child create a painting, sculpture, or wall hanging. As an adolescent, I pieced together a quilt from all of my favorite outfits from my growing-up years. How much better it would have been to have pieced together a quilt that displayed my spiritual growth or family's spiritual pilgrimage.

Since I was raised in a family where all the men were cowboys, I grew accustomed to the leather belt craft. Often, entire life stories were impressed into those belts. Use your imagination and your child's unique talents and interests and create a memorial, a tangible marker that displays when the spiritually significant events happened. The key is that the marker be permanent, something tangible that can be seen and stand as a reminder of God's grace and goodness. *Impress* God's goodness into the heart of your child.

Come, my children, listen to me;
I will teach you the fear of the Lord.
Psalm 34:11

Dear God

If we are faithless, he will remain faithful, for he cannot disown himself.
(2 Tim. 2:13)

This year, as you write a letter to thank God for all the growth He has created in you, see if you can specifically name times when He has been a shield, a fortress, a deliverer, or when He has been true to one of His names. For example, has God been a shepherd to you this year—or your provider? Thank God for always being faithful to His names.

_____

_____

_____

_____

_____

_____

_____

_____

_____

Kid Celebrations of Faith

Here is the church

Here is the steeple

Open the door

See all the people

Hear them sing!

This was one of the first songs with hand actions I learned in Sunday School. I loved going to church as I was growing up. I was the first of my family to make a commitment to Jesus. My parents didn't go to worship service when I was young. My mom did go to Sunday School, but then she took my younger brother and sister home to see my dad, a traveling non-church-going businessman. But I begged to stay for worship service, or "big church" as I called it.

I loved church. I loved the basement with colorful posters and paintings of Jesus with children. I tried to make sure I visited the kitchen every week because it always had plenty of graham crackers and red punch. I even anticipated the hallways filled with kind friendly people, many of whom were grandmothers who loved to hand out dimes to the children for no reason at all!

I loved the safe, holy feeling I would get when I sat in the sanctuary where the sun sparkled and danced through the beautiful stained-glass windows! But best of all, I loved the nursery and preschool rooms. I liked to be a helper. I loved to hold hands and play Red Rover on the grass out back. I liked to help my brother and sister and their friends learn their verses. I loved to pass out paper cups. I just loved to feel a part. I loved being a member of the church.

What does your church look like? Draw a picture:

If you could design the perfect church, one that all kids would love to come to, what would your church look like? Someday, when you get big, God might just ask you to design a church—so practice now! Ask your parents to show you what a floor plan is. When someone designs buildings for a living, he or she is called an architect. Architects create blueprints so the contractor can make sure the building is put up according to plans. Now you get to be an architect. Draw plans for a kid friendly church:

Churches are usually lead by someone called a reverend, priest, pastor, rector, vicar, or another fancy title like that. Sometimes they wear special clothes, sometimes they don't. Church leaders come in all sizes, shapes, ages. Some are men and some are women. Draw a picture of your pastor:

[Parents: this could be a senior pastor or children's director—whatever spiritual leader your child knows the best.]

If you could give your pastor some presents to make his job easier, what would they be? For example, my kids see how much their father, a pastor, is on the phone, so they might think an earphone that is tiny and hooks on sunglasses would be cool. Or they might think a watch that was also a phone, pager, and had fun computer games would be a great gift. Think of your favorite superhero cartoon. Does the superhero have some neat gadgets to catch bad guys? Draw some neat gadgets for your pastor.

How about you? What's your place in the church? Each week when we go to church, we pray that God will speak *to* us through the message or the Sunday School class. But we also pray God will speak *through* us so that someone else is encouraged, helped, or just feels better because of something nice we said or did.

Have you ever decoded a secret message? Underline every third letter and see if you get the secret message:

REYTHOLBULKANBRBGEKMIFGMJHPSDOWERNMTJHAHUNSDT

Write the letters in the spaces below.

___ ___ ___ ___ ___ ___ ___ ___ ___ ___ ___ ___ ___ ___ ___!

Yes, God thinks you are special, and you have a special place in the church! The reason why is that others are helped, encouraged, and equipped better because you are around!

The Bible tells us how to treat each other. You might have heard of the Golden Rule. It came from the Bible:

Do to others as you would have them do to you (Luke 6:31).

God has given us many guidelines to help us treat people like He would.

In English class, you have probably learned what a verb is. In the following verses, underline the verbs—the action words that tell you what to do. The first one has been done for you. These are God's ideas about how to treat people.

John 13:34
A new command I give you: <u>Love</u> one another.

Romans 12:10
Be devoted to one another in brotherly love. Honor one another above yourselves.

Romans 12:16
Live in harmony with one another. Do not be proud, but be willing to associate with people of low position. Do not be conceited.

Galatians 5:13
Serve one another in love.

Ephesians 4:2

Be completely humble and gentle; be patient, bearing with one another in love.

Ephesians 5:21

Submit to one another out of reverence for Christ.

Colossians 3:13

Bear with each other and forgive whatever grievances you may have against one another. Forgive as the Lord forgave you.

1 Thessalonians 5:11

Therefore encourage one another and build each other up, just as in fact you are doing.

Hebrews 10:24

And let us consider how we may spur one another on toward love and good deeds.

We express love and care for others in many ways. Circle the age of the people you think you make smile the easiest:

babies

preschoolers

kids my age

older kids

people my parents' age

grandparents

In our church, here are a few things that children do to serve others. Put a happy face next to any you have done before:

Set up chairs.

Walk new people to class.

Welcome new kids in class.

Pray.

Carry bundles and help teachers.

Watch little kids on the playground.

Help in the nursery.

Keep babies and little kids happy (and quiet) in big church.

Clean up after service.

Put away toys, books in the classrooms.

Hug widows and grandmas and grandpas who live far away from their families.

Help other children learn verses.

Hand out papers.

Tell others about Jesus.

Be the game leader.

Help with crafts.

Run errands for parents and teachers.

Go get little brothers and sisters from class or from the playground.

Give toys, clothes to needy children.

Help raise money for needy families or scholarships to special events.

Can you think of some people who go to your church who might be lonely or sad? Write down an idea of something you can do this week to help them feel better.

_____

_____

_____

_____

Memory Makers

Advice from Parents Who've Been There

GOD TALK ON THE GO

Sometimes passing on values and beliefs seems like an insurmountable task, especially considering the pace at which most of today's families live. When our two oldest were preschoolers, Bill and I were building a house—not having it built, rather we were the ones nailing the thing together. I was pregnant with our third, Bill was a senior pastor, working forty to fifty hours a week at a new church, and I was pitching in on ministry in a variety of ways too. Then Bill would work forty to fifty hours on the house each week also. Needless to say, it was a hectic time.

However, I developed some good spiritual habits out of necessity during that period of our life. We were committed to have dinner together regularly. I would bring it over to the lot. Then I'd pull out the Sunday School papers one of our sons had received that week at church, and we'd do family devotions from some portion of the paper over dinner. Since that time, I routinely leave the papers from church in the side pocket of my car door. When we are waiting for a sibling at a sports practice, or if we're all in the car running errands, I'll pull out the papers and we'll sing a song from them, read the Bible story or true-life story, or talk about the principle in the lesson.

I also carry *Choices*, a kids' card game (and now *Teen Choices* too), in the glove compartment, and as we travel we'll talk about how God would want us to handle choices that come at us in life. *Ungame* questions and *Bible Trivia* questions are other games that have passed through my glove compartment. Often a child's teachable moment is when you are on the go! It would be easy to guesstimate the average time a child is in the car—probably close to 364 hours per year or more! That means between the ages of one and sixteen (when the driver's license is given in most states), you and your child have the potential for over five thousand hours of spiritual conversations on the go! This is a lot of "God talk!"

KiD QUOTES!

"One Sunday night, I gave my young son a dollar bill to place in the offering plate at church. As the usher handed him the plate full of bills, he very politely looked up and said, 'No thank you, I already have one.'"
—*Connie Bennage, Pennsylvania* [1]

MY QUOTES!

_____

_____

_____

_____

_____

_____

_____

_____

_____

_____

_____

_____

1. *Today's Christian Woman*, September/October 1995, 43.

Happy Spiritual Birthday to You!

My friends Jerry and Patti MacGregor have hundreds of great family ideas in their book *Family Times: Growing Together in Fun and Faith*. Several ideas in their chapter on building a child's self-esteem are ideas that our family has also enjoyed—and adapted to mark spiritually significant moments. Below is one idea: a Coat of Arms. On construction paper, draw a coat of arms. Then have your child draw pictures in each section according to the following instructions.

Section one (top left): Draw your favorite place in the whole world.

Section two (top right): Draw your favorite memory of the last year.

Section three (bottom left): Draw a picture of something special that happened at church this year.

Section four (bottom right): Write your favorite verse or ask your parents if there is a verse that summarizes your past year, then print it in your very best printing!

Dear God

Let us not give up meeting together, as some are in the habit of doing, but let us encourage one another—and all the more as you see the Day approaching.
(Heb. 10:25)

Have you ever read a letter to the editor? In the newspaper, there is a section where people share their opinions and beliefs with each other. People write to the editor, the person in charge, and let the editor know how they feel about important topics. This year, in your letter to God section, write a letter to the editor and explain why you think it is important for people to: (1) grow in their relationship with God by reading the Bible daily; (2) grow by attending church regularly. The letter has been started for you.

Dear Editor:

REFLECTIONS

Now it is your turn, as the parent(s), to explain why you are connected to other people who believe. As you reflect on the growth and change your son or daughter has had in his or her life this year, you might also ask people whom your family worships with to write a sentence or two, and incorporate their reflections about your child as well. One way is to interview them by phone or in person and simply get a quote from them, then incorporate the quotes into your reflective writing about the past year.

_____

_____

_____

_____

_____

_____

_____

_____

_____

_____

_____

_____

_____

_____

_____

_____

_____

_____

One generation will commend your works to another;
they will tell of your mighty acts.
Psalm 145:4

Kid Celebrations of Faith

We can get to know even more about Jesus through reading and studying the Bible. When you have a best friend, you want to know all about him or her, right? Well we can know all about Jesus by reading the book God wrote for us. The Bible is an amazing book. Here are some amazing facts about the Bible:

- 66 books
- Written over a 1,500-year span
- Written over 40 generations
- Written by over 40 authors from every walk of life including kings, peasants, philosophers, fishermen, poets, statesmen, and scholars
- Written in three languages (Hebrew, Aramaic, and Greek)[1]

And what is so amazing is that all those words give the same message of God's love and forgiveness to people. Sometimes everyone in your family can't even agree on where to eat dinner, but all the people God used to write the Bible agreed with each other, and the message of God's grace to us was given over many years, using many people, in many languages. The Bible is amazing because "All scripture is given by inspiration of God" (2 Tim. 3:16, KJV). God used men to write His Word, so it is different than any other book because, really, God is the author!

God took very careful care of the Bible. It has come on a long journey from when it was first written to the Bible that you have. On page 60 is a chart, showing the journey the Bible has taken. There are empty boxes that have pieces of the journey that need to be filled in. With every box is a number, and it connects to each of the numbered pieces of the Bible's journey, starting on the next page. In the box draw a picture of what is described so you can see the amazing journey the Bible has come on.

---

1. Josh McDowell, *Evidence That Demands a Verdict*, (San Bernardino, CA: Here's Life Publishers, 1979) 16.

1 Remember God wrote the Ten Commandments on a stone, with His own finger. But Israel was disobedient, and when Moses went down from the mountain where he was meeting with God, he saw the people worshiping a golden calf. Moses was very upset and threw the tablets down and they broke. God had him chisel them again into the stone tablets.

2 Look up Exodus 20:3-17 and write the Ten Commandments on the tablets below in your own words. The first one has been done for you. In box 2, you might draw the outline of the tablets.

1. Worship only the Lord as God.

3 As God would speak to His leaders, they would write down His words on scrolls of papyrus. (This was an early form of paper. It would be in long rolls, kind of like paper towels or wrapping paper comes today.) The scrolls were kept in God's holy places of worship—at first in the ark of the covenant, then the ark was placed in the tabernacle, then the temple. Later, copies of scrolls were placed in churches and monasteries (places where church leaders lived and worshiped). In box 3, you might draw a scroll.

4 One day, soldiers (draw a soldier) were coming to destroy the temple so the scrolls were hidden in a cave.

5 Some people had copies of God's Word, so church leaders would make new Bibles by carefully copying word-for-word every word and every punctuation mark in the Bible. This took a very long time to do. Look at your Bible. How long do you think it would take you to copy every word in it? Write how long you think it would take you: _____.

Because it took so long, only a few church leaders had their own Bibles. In fact most pastors, monks, and ministers didn't have their own Bibles. It got very hard to lead the people in truth when they didn't know the truth. People began to mix in their own beliefs with the Bible teaching they had heard from these confused leaders. The world became a very mixed-up place. History calls this the Dark Ages. I believe it was so dark because people didn't have their own Bibles and there was no light to live by. God's Word says: *Your word is a lamp to my feet and a light for my path* (Ps. 119:105). People didn't have the Word, so they didn't have the light and they made some poor choices and bad decisions.

One bad decision was that the leaders decided they never wanted the people to have their own Bibles. But some courageous men, known as reformers, thought all people should have their own Bibles. Some of these men were Martin Luther, John Wycliffe, and William Tyndale. Wycliffe and Tyndale did everything they could to get copies of the Bible into the hands of everyday people. A man named Johannes Gutenberg invented the printing press and printed a Bible on it. Bibles could be copied much faster on the press. Many people risked their lives to smuggle Bibles and get them to the people. The law said people could not print Bibles, sell Bibles, or own Bibles. But these brave people did everything they could to get Bibles to people—ones that were translated into their own language so they could easily read and understand them.

6 Sometimes people would hide copies of the Bible in rolls of fabric or inside their hats! If someone wanted to take your Bible, where would you hide it?

_____

These brave leaders went to jail, and many of them were killed. They believed it was worth it. Getting the Bible into each person's hands was a very important goal that God wanted them to do. They did get the Bible into the hands of many, many people. The laws finally changed in many countries so people could legally own Bibles in their own language. How does knowing what all these brave people went through make you feel about your own Bible? Write how you will treat your Bible:

_____

_____

7 Oh, and remember those scrolls that were hidden in a cave? Not long ago, a shepherd boy found them, and guess what? The words are the same as in the Bible you have. That's amazing! The Bible has been translated into many languages. It is often translated and made easier for children to read. Remember to draw a picture of your Bible!

The Bible is very precious, very important. It is more important than all your favorite toys or games. Draw a picture of your favorite toys or games.

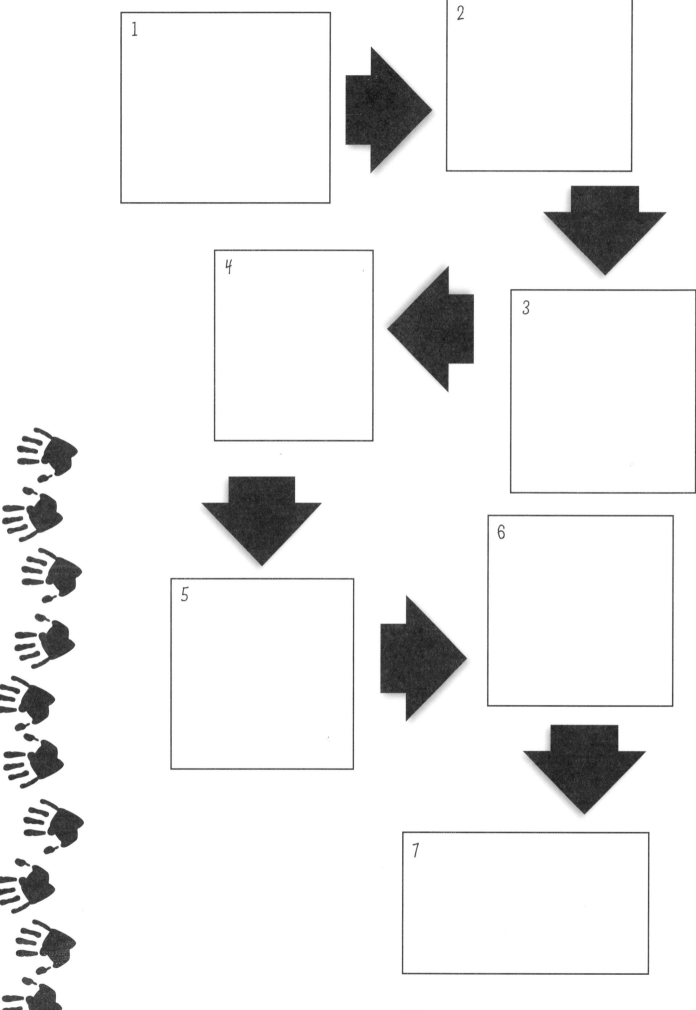

MY QUOTES!

2. *Today's Christian Woman*, November/December 1999, 24.

Happy Spiritual Birthday to You!

My first writing job was for a newspaper. I spent a year jamming out stories. Some of them actually made the front page! This year, mark your child's spiritual growth by creating a front page for your child. This is one of my favorite ideas, and each family member I have done it for has enjoyed not only the moment the gift is given, but the lasting impact of having a framed copy including a picture of him, hanging in his room. You say you're not a journalist, not to worry. Just answer the following questions, and it should help get you started on a super article about your child. What were the highlights of the year? Where did she travel (conferences, field trips, and so on)? What helped him grow? Interview a couple of your child's friends. Ask: *What do you think is his/her best trait? How has he/she reflected God's character this year (has she/he done anything extra special or nice)?* Then casually interview your child: *Honey, what have you learned about God this year? Do you remember any time this past year you think God spoke to you through His Word, and you obeyed what He asked? How do you feel about God? For example, if I asked you to write a commercial for God, what would you say?*

These questions should give you enough information to pull an article together. You might write several short paragraphs under one headline, and do that a couple of times to make the page layout more interesting. By using columns, you can use the words to frame graphics or photographs of your child to complete the page. Make sure you have a flashy headline, then frame it and present it to your child on the date of his or her spiritual birthday or other significant day for your child. There's not much more exciting in life than making the news!

A variation of this would be to create a video news magazine piece on your child. Interview his or her friends, teachers, pastors or other spiritual leaders, then add your own commentary. You can take photographs to a video service, have them add some music, and you have a spiritual birthday heirloom!

Dear God

Read the following verses and circle every time *word* appears. Now read the verses again and write a letter to God. Tell Him why His Word is precious to you. See if you can remember times this past year when a particular verse might have answered a question, guided you, or helped you obey

Psalm 33:4
For the word of the Lord is right and true;
he is faithful in all he does.

Psalm 119:9
How can a young man keep his way pure?
By living according to your word.

Psalm 119:11
I have hidden your word in my heart
that I might not sin against you.

Psalm 119:16
I delight in your decrees;
I will not neglect your word.

Psalm 119:28
My soul is weary with sorrow;
strengthen me according to your word.

Psalm 119:37
Turn my eyes away from worthless things;
preserve my life according to your word.

Psalm 119:89
Your word, O Lord, is eternal;
it stands firm in the heavens.

Psalm 119:105
Your word is a lamp to my feet
and a light for my path.

Psalm 119:114
You are my refuge and my shield;
I have put my hope in your word.

Psalm 119:133
Direct my footsteps according to your word;
let no sin rule over me.

REFLECTIONS

This year, share some of the verses you have been praying for your child, or choose some verses and string them together to pray for your child in the coming year. Here's an example:

Let those who love the Lord hate evil, for he guards the lives of his faithful ones.[3] *My son, if sinners entice you, do not give in to them.*[4] *May you be as Daniel, who so distinguished himself among the administrators and the satraps by his exceptional qualities that the king planned to set him over the whole kingdom.*[5] *My prayer is not that you take them out of the world but that you protect them from the evil one.*[6] *Therefore, I urge you, brothers, in view of God's mercy, to offer your bodies as living sacrifices, holy and pleasing to God—this is your spiritual act of worship. Do not conform any longer to the pattern of this world, but be transformed by the renewing of your mind. Then you will be able to test and approve what God's will is—his good, pleasing and perfect will.*[7] *Everyone must submit himself to the governing authorities, for there is no authority except that which God has established. The authorities that exist have been established by God.*[8] *Flee from sexual immorality. All other sins a man commits are outside his body, but he who sins sexually sins against his own body. Do you not know that your body is a temple of the Holy Spirit, who is in you, whom you have received from God? You are not your own; you were bought at a price. Therefore honor God with your body.*[9] *Do not be yoked together with unbelievers. For what do righteousness and wickedness have in common? Or what fellowship can light have with darkness?*[10] *Submit yourselves, then, to God. Resist the devil, and he will flee from you.*[11]

Even when I am old and gray,

do not forsake me, O God,

till I declare your power to the next generation,

your might to all who are to come.

Psalm 71:18

---

3. Psalm 97:10, 4. Proverbs 1:10, 5. Daniel 6:3, 6. John 17:15, 7. Romans 12:1-2, 8. Romans 13:1, 9. 1 Corinthians 6:18-20, 10. 2 Corinthians 6:14, 11. James 4:7

Celebrate! God Is a Friend to Children

It's a Party!
Kid Celebrations of Faith

Have you ever wondered if a young person could be a friend to God? You can! There are some great stories about some great kids in the Bible! Stories about God's friendships with these young people are sprinkled all through the Bible.

A BOY KING

Did you know there was a boy who became king of a whole country when he was only eight years old? Below is a description of him as a man. Underline his name and anything that is positive (good) about him.

> Furthermore, Josiah got rid of the mediums and spiritists *[people that followed dark worship, kind of like witches]*, the household gods *[statues and other objects people worshiped instead of the true God of the Bible]*, the idols and all the other detestable things seen in Judah and Jerusalem. This he did to fulfill the requirements of the law written in the book that Hilkiah the priest had discovered in the temple of the Lord. Neither before nor after Josiah was there a king like him who turned to the Lord as he did—with all his heart and with all his soul and with all his strength, in accordance with all the Law of Moses (2 Kings 23:24-25).
>
> Josiah removed all the detestable idols *[false gods]* from all the territory belonging to the Israelites, and he had all who were present in Israel serve the Lord their God. As long as he lived, they did not fail to follow the Lord, the God of their fathers. (2 Chron. 34:33). *[Explanations added.]*

King Josiah took a stand against evil. What are some things that are wrong, or bad for you that you can speak up against, even though you are young? (For example: illegal drugs, violent gangs, cruel teasing) _____

_____

_____

_____

THREE BRAVE FRIENDS

There were also three friends, Shadrach, Meshach, and Abednego, all friends of Daniel. These young men all worshiped the true God. Read the story below and put a happy face by anything that describes good and a sad face by anything that is mean, bad, or evil.

Moreover, at Daniel's request the king appointed Shadrach, Meshach and Abednego administrators over the province of Babylon, while Daniel himself remained at the royal court (Dan. 2:49). "But there are some Jews whom you have set over the affairs of the province of Babylon—Shadrach, Meshach and Abednego—who pay no attention to you, O king. They neither serve your gods nor worship the image of gold you have set up."

Furious with rage, Nebuchadnezzar summoned Shadrach, Meshach and Abednego. So these men were brought before the king, and Nebuchadnezzar said to them, "Is it true, Shadrach, Meshach and Abednego, that you do not serve my gods or worship the image of gold I have set up?" (Dan. 3:12-14)

Shadrach, Meshach and Abednego replied to the king, "O Nebuchadnezzar, we do not need to defend ourselves before you in this matter" (Dan. 3:16). Then Nebuchadnezzar was furious with Shadrach, Meshach and Abednego, and his attitude toward them changed. He ordered the furnace heated seven times hotter than usual and commanded some of the strongest soldiers in his army to tie up Shadrach, Meshach and Abednego and throw them into the blazing furnace.... The king's command was so urgent and the furnace so hot that the flames of the fire killed the soldiers who took up Shadrach, Meshach and Abednego, and these three men, firmly tied, fell into the blazing furnace. Then King Nebuchadnezzar leaped to his feet in amazement and asked his advisers, "Weren't there three men that we tied up and threw into the fire?"

They replied, "Certainly, O king."

He said, "Look! I see four men walking around in the fire, unbound and unharmed, and the fourth looks like a son of the gods."

Nebuchadnezzar then approached the opening of the blazing furnace and shouted, "Shadrach, Meshach and Abednego, servants of the Most High God, come out! Come here!"

So Shadrach, Meshach and Abednego came out of the fire, and the satraps, prefects, governors and royal advisers crowded around them. They saw that the fire had not harmed their bodies, nor was a hair of their heads singed; their robes were not scorched, and there was no smell of fire on them.

Then Nebuchadnezzar said, "Praise be to the God of Shadrach, Meshach and Abednego, who has sent his angel and rescued his servants! They trusted in him and defied the king's command and were willing to give up their lives rather than serve or worship any god except their own God. Therefore I decree that the people of any nation or language who say anything against the God of Shadrach, Meshach and Abednego be cut into pieces and their houses be turned into piles of rubble, for no other god can save in this way."

Then the king promoted Shadrach, Meshach, and Abednego in the province of Babylon.

KING NEBUCHADNEZZAR,

To the peoples, nations and men of every language, who live in all the world: May you prosper greatly! It is my pleasure to tell you about the miraculous signs and wonders that the Most High God has performed for me. How great are his signs, how mighty his wonders! His kingdom is an eternal kingdom; *his dominion endures from generation to generation* (Dan. 3:19–4:3). (Emphasis added.)

The New Testament tells us to overcome evil with good (Rom. 12:21). It is good to have friends who also will stand with you for God against evil. Who are your strongest Christian friends? _____

_____

STANDING ALONE FOR WHAT IS GOOD

Daniel also stood tall and proud for God. He was such a good leader that the king planned to make him number-two man in the kingdom. Some of the other leaders got jealous and tried to find a way to discredit and destroy Daniel. But these men couldn't find anything wrong; Daniel was a man with integrity! So the mean men tricked the king into writing a new law, one that would punish anyone who would not bow and pray to the king as if he was a god. Daniel would not pray to the king, but only to the true God. Every day he prayed and people could see him in his window. This made the king's leaders angry, so they talked the king into throwing Daniel into the lions' den. Daniel was put into a den of hungry lions, but God kept the mouths of the lions shut! Daniel was safe! (Dan. 6:1-28) Daniel was rewarded and the mean men were punished.

People could see Daniel praying in his room by looking in his window. Draw a picture of your house and draw a picture of the window to your room and place yourself in the window praying to God.

CONFIDENT QUEEN

Esther was a brave princess. She risked her life to save God's people. (Read all about her in the Book of Esther). One of the smartest things Esther did was to obey her uncle. She was young when she was named queen, so she relied on her uncle's wisdom to help her. Esther didn't have parents, so her uncle Mordecai raised her, and Esther respected him very much. Her uncle also loved God. Mordecai came to her and told her to ask the king to save God's people. Esther was very afraid, but she did another smart thing. Read these verses. What is the smart thing she did?

> Then Esther sent this reply to Mordecai: "Go, gather together all the Jews who are in Susa, and fast for me. Do not eat or drink for three days, night or day. I and my maids will fast as you do. When this is done, I will go to the king, even though it is against the law. And if I perish, I perish" (Es. 4:15-16).

Esther was a praying princess. She asked others to pray for her. Who prays for you?

_____

LISTENING FOR GOD'S CALL

Samuel was just a kid when he came to live at the temple with Eli the priest so he could learn to serve God. Samuel was a miracle baby. His mom, Hannah, could not have a baby for a very, very long time. She was very, very sad. She came to the temple (God's house, like a church) and prayed. She promised God something. Read the verse below and find the promise she made. Underline the promise.

> Hannah was very sad. She cried much and prayed to the Lord. She made a promise. She said, "Lord of heaven's armies, see how bad I feel. Remember me! Don't forget me. If you will give me a son, I will give him back to you all his life" (1 Sam. 1:10-11, NCV).

God heard her prayer and gave her a baby, Samuel. When he was very small he came to live with Eli at the temple. God wanted to use Samuel in a very special and important way, but first Samuel had to learn to listen for God's voice. Read the story on the next page. Every time you think it's God talking, circle those words by drawing a cloud around them like this:

Then the Lord called Samuel.

Samuel answered, "Here I am." And he ran to Eli and said, "Here I am; you called me."

But Eli said, "I did not call; go back and lie down." So he went and lay down.

Again the Lord called, "Samuel!" And Samuel got up and went to Eli and said, "Here I am; you called me."

"My son," Eli said, "I did not call; go back and lie down."

Now Samuel did not yet know the Lord: The word of the Lord had not yet been revealed to him.

The Lord called Samuel a third time, and Samuel got up and went to Eli and said, "Here I am; you called me."

Then Eli realized that the Lord was calling the boy. So Eli told Samuel, "Go and lie down, and if he calls you, say, 'Speak, Lord, for your servant is listening.'" So Samuel went and lay down in his place.

The Lord came and stood there, calling as at the other times, "Samuel! Samuel!"

Then Samuel said, "Speak, for your servant is listening" (1 Sam. 3:4-10).

We also need to learn to listen to God. After you read the Bible, don't just run out and play. Try not to have the radio or TV on when you are reading the Bible. Instead read, then wait just a few seconds, and pray, *God teach me*, or *God, Your turn*, or *God, speak to my heart*. Tell God you are listening. God loves a listening heart. In the verses below, draw a heart above the word *heart* each time it appears.

Psalm 13:5
But I trust in your unfailing love;
my heart rejoices in your salvation.

Psalm 19:14
May the words of my mouth
and the meditation of my heart
be pleasing in your sight,
O Lord, my Rock and my Redeemer.

Psalm 26:2-3
Test me, O Lord, and try me,
examine my heart and my mind;
for your love is ever before me,
and I walk continually in your truth.

Psalm 27:8
My heart says of you, "Seek his face!"
Your face, Lord, I will seek.

COURAGEOUS SHEPHERD BOY

David was also just a kid when God selected him to be the next king. God sent Samuel to a house with many sons. David was the youngest, just a shepherd boy. Samuel thought God wanted to choose the strongest, oldest, most handsome. But God told Samuel the right son was the smallest, David. God said: "The Lord does not look at the things man looks at. Man looks at the outward appearance, but the Lord looks at the heart" (1 Sam. 16:7). The Bible says about David, "The Lord has sought out a man after his own heart and appointed him leader of his people" (1 Sam.13:14).

David was also very brave. A giant was tormenting and defeating God's army. Everyone was afraid—except David. (Read all about it in 1 Samuel 17.) David came to bring supplies, but ended up taking on the giant without any armor or the regular weapons—just five small stones! David wasn't afraid because he knew God. He had spent time praying and singing to God as he watched the sheep. The giant, Goliath, was making fun of David. David replied, "You come against me with sword and spear and javelin, but I come against you in the name of the Lord Almighty, the God of the armies of Israel, whom you have defied" (1 Sam. 17:45). Then David put a stone in a sling and flung it at the giant. CRASH! Down the giant fell! The people cheered for David! In the space below, either draw a picture of you cheering for God and the cheer you would say, or draw a picture of David defeating the giant.

David loved God very much. He expressed his love for God by writing songs and poems to God. They are called psalms. In the psalm below, draw a crown over any time it talks about how good God is. What other words in this psalm could you draw a picture over to get a better idea what David is saying? Try it!

Psalm 23: A Psalm of David.

The Lord is my shepherd, I shall not be in want.

He makes me lie down in green pastures,

he leads me beside quiet waters,

he restores my soul.

He guides me in paths of righteousness

for his name's sake.

Even though I walk

through the valley of the shadow of death,

I will fear no evil,

for you are with me;

your rod and your staff,

they comfort me.

You prepare a table before me

in the presence of my enemies.

You anoint my head with oil;

my cup overflows.

Surely goodness and love will follow me

all the days of my life,

and I will dwell in the house of the Lord forever.

Try your hand at your own poem! Rewrite a poem, like this:

Roses are red

Violets are blue

Every word in the Bible

Is definitely true!

Or create an original!

_____

_____

_____

_____

KiD QUotes!

"The other day my husband was driving our two year old, Bryan, and our five-year-old daughter, Brooke, home from day care. Brooke said, 'Daddy, today I prayed for two more sisters and another brother.' My husband replied that it would be nice to have a larger family, but gently explained it probably wouldn't happen. Brooke, who was seated behind him in the car, leaned forward and whispered in his ear, 'How do you think I got Bryan?'"
—*Kari Voight, Minnesota*[1]

MY QUotes!

_____

_____

_____

_____

_____

_____

_____

1. *Today's Christian Woman*, September/October 1997, 37.

Happy Spiritual Birthday to You!

In Old Testament times, when a father wanted to pass on his heritage, he would pronounce a blessing over the child. (See Genesis 49:28 and following.) This was a father's way to prophesy what he thought was ahead for the child in life. (Gary Smalley and John Trent made the giving of a blessing a popular activity through their practical book *The Blessing.*)

In our home, every Thanksgiving and Christmas, each person sitting around our table, including our sons, receives a blessing from Bill and me. We stand to the person's side, lay a hand on his shoulder, and bend to look him in the eye. We also have small candles on each plate and after the blessing we light his candle. (It's a big deal at our house when we let the children light their own candles—this means they are growing up!)

We use this time to compliment character and to give our hope for the future. For example, a blessing might sound like this: *Brock, we have seen God use your life and your love of sports to bring new life to so many of your friends this year. We are confident that God who began a good work in you will complete it. We anticipate more exciting things in the year ahead. May God continue to honor you, son, because you have chosen to honor Him. We love you and we are proud to call you our son.*

You can make these blessings permanent by recording them in this book, by turning them into posters, bookmarks, or frame the blessing. We are very fortunate; each of our sons marks his spiritual birthday by a holiday. Brock gave his life to God on Father's Day, Zach on Mother's Day, and Caleb on Easter. We've chosen to remember each son in some special, sometimes small, ways on those dates. Some years, we choose to turn the blessing into a prayer for that child. A nice gesture is when the whole family joins in and prays for that one child.

The blessing can also be as simple as a birthday card with a personalized prayer written on the inside then tucked under a pillow or in a backpack.

Dear God

Enoch walked with God (Gen. 5:24). *Noah was a righteous man, blameless among the people of his time, and he walked with God* (Gen. 6:9). *When Abram was ninety-nine years old, the Lord appeared to him and said, "I am God Almighty; walk before me and be blameless* (Gen. 17:1). *In the land of Uz there lived a man whose name was Job. This man was blameless and upright; he feared God and shunned evil* (Job 1:1).

Would you like to be a friend to God like Enoch, Abram, Job, and Noah? Remember the young people who loved God: David, Joseph, Daniel and his friends, Esther, and Josiah? Tell God thanks for teaching you how to be His friend this year. Then write a description of what a best friend is (loyal, faithful, a listener, and so on). Let God know you want to be His friend. God will always be there for you; you can choose to be there, walking with God your whole life—one step at a time.

_____

_____

_____

_____

_____

_____

_____

_____

_____

_____

REFLECTIONS

This year, take a good look at your child's friendships. What are his or her best interpersonal relationship qualities? How could these qualities enhance his or her friendship with God? As you reflect back on the spiritual growth of your child, compliment relational skills and connect him or her to God by helping your child see how he or she is, and can be, a friend to God.

_____

_____

_____

_____

_____

_____

_____

_____

_____

_____

_____

_____

_____

_____

Then we your people, the sheep of your pasture,

will praise you forever;

from generation to generation

we will recount your praise.

Psalm 79:13

It's a Party!
Kid Celebrations of Faith

In the children's fairy tale "Snow White," there is a wicked witch. Every day, she looks into the mirror on her wall and says, "Mirror, Mirror, on the wall; who's the fairest of them all?" She wants to hear the mirror's opinion of who is best. Sometimes we do the same thing. We look to friends, TV shows, and magazines to decide what is cool, in, acceptable—and even to decide if we are acceptable. But God has a better plan. It is a much better idea to let God be your mirror. God is all knowing, and He sees the truth about everything—even us—all the time.

So if you are feeling bad about yourself, quit looking at the bathroom mirror! Look in God's Word! If you are wondering if something is good or bad, right or wrong, don't just ask your friends—look in God's Word!

God's Word is a mirror of truth. Satan will want to trip you up with lies. You'll hear things like, *Oh, that was stupid! Can't you do anything right? You are so dumb!* And sometime you might hear things even more hurtful than these statements. These kinds of lies sting worse than any bee sting. These words hurt our heart. But these unkind and cruel statements are lies, and you need to protect your mind from lies.

God tells us how to protect our mind from lies:

Ephesians 4:22-24
You were taught, with regard to your former way of life, to put off your old self, which is being corrupted by its deceitful desires; to be made new in the attitude of your minds; and to put on the new self, created to be like God in true righteousness and holiness.

Underline the words *put off* and *put on*. This means you can *choose* to leave the lies and choose to learn to listen to God's truth.

Colossians 3:2
Set your minds on things above, not on earthly things.

What are the things above? Read Philippians 4:8 and make a list of things for each one of the words that describe the good things God wants us to think about:

Philippians 4:8
Finally, brothers, [Or sisters, moms, or dads!]
whatever is true, [Facts are true. List some facts about God that are true that you've learned so far in **Celebrate!**] _____

_____

whatever is noble, [Queens and kings are nobility. List other people you can look up to as a good role model.] _____

_____

whatever is right, [Obeying the law is right. Can you think of rules, laws, or guidelines that have helped you or made your life safe?] _____

_____

whatever is pure, [Snow is pure—well almost! God's love is pure—totally!] _____

_____

whatever is lovely, [Roses are lovely. What else is beautiful?] _____

_____

whatever is admirable [Great art, good books, yummy food are a few admirable things— what else can you think of?] _____

_____

—if anything is excellent or praiseworthy [Now just list all your favorite things!] _____

_____

think about such things. [So next time you are grumpy, feeling bad about yourself, or just woke up on the wrong side of the bed, think on these things and you can have a change of attitude!]

1 Peter 1:13

Therefore, prepare your minds for action; be self-controlled; set your hope fully on the grace to be given you when Jesus Christ is revealed.

Circle the word *action*. That word is the picture of being ready for battle. When people are in the military, they have everything ready, all the time, just in case the enemy attacks. That's what God wants us to do with our minds—be ready when the lies attack—have a plan, like the one you just created from Philippians 4:8!

2 Corinthians 10:5

We demolish arguments and every pretension that sets itself up against the knowledge of God, and we take captive every thought to make it obedient to Christ.

Circle the word *demolish*. Have you ever watched fireworks explode in the sky? That's what God wants to do to the arguments (lies against Him). He explodes them with the truth until the lie is completely gone.

Now circle the words *take captive*. This is the picture of a good guy locking up a bad guy. God takes the bad thoughts and puts them in jail so they can't hurt you anymore!

Draw a picture of a good guy locking the bad guy in jail. Now write the words "Bad thoughts are locked away from me by God!" underneath, as in a comic strip.

Now when a bad, mean, cruel, or untrue thought comes into your head, you know what to do. You can tell yourself: *God is stronger than this thought. This thought is wrong and I will lock it away. I will not think about it anymore. Jesus, thank You for shedding Your blood on the cross to set me free from Satan and his lies. Now I will think on the truth.* Then think of something good off the Philippians 4:8 list!

When you give your thought life to Jesus, God's Holy Spirit is in control of your thoughts instead of the bad lies. Read Romans 8:6: "The mind of sinful man is death, but the mind controlled by the Spirit is life and peace." What are the payoffs if you give your thought life to the Spirit of God? Underline the two benefits at the end of the sentence and write them here: _____ and _____! Those are two very good things!

We can give the Holy Spirit control of our hearts moment by moment. When we walk with God, God will let us know when we do something that doesn't please Him. It's like He says, "That's wrong." And we have a choice at that point. We can keep doing it our way, the wrong way. God doesn't move or change. HE is still God, but we walk away from Him and His plan for us. But all you have to do is agree with Him that it was wrong. (That's called confess your sins.) Then ask Him to control your life again and thank Him for His Spirit's leading. You and God can keep walking together in the plans He has for you.

When we walk in the power of the Holy Spirit, we start to see things differently, closer to God's point of view. God wants us to see *ourselves* from His point of view too. In the New Testament, there are many places that God says, "You are . . ." and He completes a sentence and tells us some things that are true about those of us who have a personal relationship with Him. Look at the mirror on the next page and read some of the *You Ares*. These are just a few—but these are some great ones to start remembering about yourself! This is how God sees you!

Family specialist Dr. Kevin Leman notes, "One of the most cherished values in our family is faith. From what I have seen behind counseling doors, there is no better builder of self image and a sense of self-worth than to know that you are the handiwork of an all-powerful Creator. . ." [1]

---

1. Kevin Leman, *Brining Up Kids Without Tearing Them Down,* (Nashville: Thomas Nelson, 1995) 66.

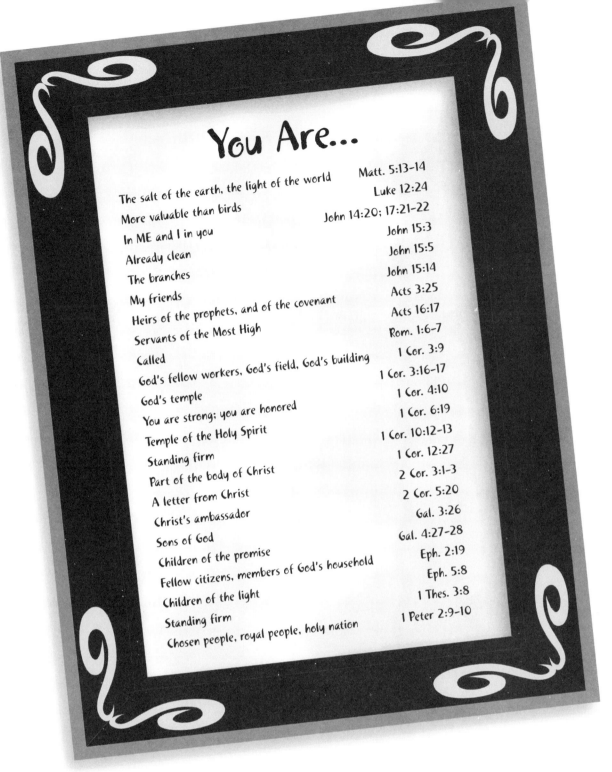

You Are...

The salt of the earth, the light of the world	Matt. 5:13-14
More valuable than birds	Luke 12:24
In ME and I in you	John 14:20; 17:21-22
Already clean	John 15:3
The branches	John 15:5
My friends	John 15:14
Heirs of the prophets, and of the covenant	Acts 3:25
Servants of the Most High	Acts 16:17
Called	Rom. 1:6-7
God's fellow workers, God's field, God's building	1 Cor. 3:9
God's temple	1 Cor. 3:16-17
You are strong; you are honored	1 Cor. 4:10
Temple of the Holy Spirit	1 Cor. 6:19
Standing firm	1 Cor. 10:12-13
Part of the body of Christ	1 Cor. 12:27
A letter from Christ	2 Cor. 3:1-3
Christ's ambassador	2 Cor. 5:20
Sons of God	Gal. 3:26
Children of the promise	Gal. 4:27-28
Fellow citizens, members of God's household	Eph. 2:19
Children of the light	Eph. 5:8
Standing firm	1 Thes. 3:8
Chosen people, royal people, holy nation	1 Peter 2:9-10

Which one is your favorite?
In the blank mirror to the right,
write which one you like best,
and why you like it.

KiD QUotes!

"Shortly after our family began having nightly family devotions—which isn't easy with a precocious four-year-old daughter and an impish two-year-old son—my daughter asked, 'Mommy, when are we gonna get together with Daddy and Austin to talk to God and have family commotions?'"
—*Carla Crumley-Forest, Florida*[2]

MY QUotes!

_____

_____

_____

_____

_____

_____

_____

_____

_____

2. *Today's Christian Woman*, May/ June 1995, 33.

Happy Spiritual Birthday to You!

This year, begin introducing your child to spiritual leaders in history. Buy a biography and frame an inspirational quote, or have a pencil holder, clock, or other practical item engraved with a quote. My son Caleb has a heart for righteousness. He makes sure life runs according to the rules. He hates injustice. Knowing this (and the fact that I think Dr. Martin Luther King's "I Have a Dream" speech is one of the best in history) I bought Caleb a copy of the illustrated children's version of that speech. I wrote a full-page letter in the flyleaf of the book to Caleb, complimenting his love for justice and righteousness. I added that because Caleb valued those qualities, if he kept growing in Christ that someday, I thought God would use some of Caleb's words to correct an injustice or change society.

An easy way to find quotes by famous people is to log onto the Internet, plug in the keyword *quotes* and you will discover all kinds of sites that are nothing but quotes! Many of these offer a search option where you can plug in a word and quotes containing that word will appear. You can also search by author.

Here are a few quotes about the Bible by famous people in history:

• George Washington: "It is impossible to rightly govern the world without God and the Bible."

• John Quincy Adams: "So great is my veneration of the Bible, that the earlier my children begin to read it the more confident will be my hope that they will prove useful citizens of their country and respectable members of society."

• Charles Dickens: "The New Testament is the very best book that ever was or ever will be known in the world."

• Andrew Jackson: "That book, sir, is the rock on which our republic rests."

• Abraham Lincoln: "I believe the Bible is the best gift God has ever given to man. All the good from the Savior of the world is communicated to us through this book."

• Horace Greeley: "It is impossible to mentally or socially enslave a Bible-reading people. The principles of the Bible are the groundwork of human freedom."

· Woodrow Wilson: "I ask every man and woman in this audience that from this day on they will realize that part of the destiny of America lies in their daily perusal of this great Book."

· Douglas MacArthur: "Believe me, sir, never a night goes by, be I ever so tired, but I read the Word of God before I go to bed."

· Herbert Hoover: "The whole of the inspiration of our civilization springs from the teachings of Christ and the lessons of the Prophets. To read the Bible for these fundamentals is a necessity of American life.

· Dwight D. Eisenhower: "To read the Bible is to take a trip to a fair land where the spirit is strengthened and faith renewed." [3]

Dear God

The Beatitudes

Blessed are the poor in spirit,
for theirs is the kingdom of heaven.
Blessed are those who mourn,
for they will be comforted.
Blessed are the meek,
for they will inherit the earth.
Blessed are those who hunger and thirst for righteousness,
for they will be filled.
Blessed are the merciful,
for they will be shown mercy.
Blessed are the pure in heart,
for they will see God.
Blessed are the peacemakers,
for they will be called sons of God.
Blessed are those who are persecuted because of righteousness,
for theirs is the kingdom of heaven.
Blessed are you when people insult you, persecute you and falsely say all kinds of evil
against you because of me (Matt. 5:3-11).

3. Pam Farrel, *30 Ways to Wake Up Your Quiet* (Downers Grove, IL: InterVarsity Press 1999), p. 11. Originally from *Tans Encyclopedia 7700 Illustrations,* WordSearch, NavPress, # 419.

This is a part of Jesus' Sermon on the Mount. Jesus is telling the people that they will be blessed (which means happy, fulfilled, content, peaceful) if they walk according to God's priorities in life. You will have a better life if you look at life the same way God does. Earlier, you looked at how God sees you. This is how God sees life. Read the Beatitudes again and underline the kind of people that God blesses. For example, *"Blessed are the poor in spirit, for theirs is the kingdom of heaven. Poor in spirit* doesn't mean they are poor, like with no money; instead it means they have a humble attitude. These people aren't all bragging and thinking they are hot stuff. They put the feelings of others first.

Write a letter to Jesus, and tell Him what you learned from the Beatitudes, and from the "Mirror, Mirror" section in the first part of the chapter. Tell God some of your happy memories from the year and see if you can link them back to one of the Beatitudes. For example, When I was in fifth grade, I won "Best Smile" in my class. This was especially meaningful to me because when I was in third grade, my little brother, who was jumping on the bed, accidentally jumped on to my head while I was talking and broke my front tooth. The dentist couldn't fix it! I had to have a broken front tooth for five years! I remember thinking, *I just will never smile again!* But then my mother, my family, and friends all reminded me that I had a lot to smile about. I had a home, food, good grades. This was about the same time I learned the Beatitudes, and I realized that life with God gave me something to smile about! So I smiled at everyone—all the time! I wanted to forget my broken tooth and focus on making others happy—and that made me happy!

_____

_____

_____

_____

_____

_____

_____

_____

_____

REFLECTIONS

When we grow up, sometimes life in our homes is less than perfect. Sometimes the messages we are given as children aren't true messages at all. Maybe when you where a child you heard you were no good, couldn't do anything right, a drain on your parents—or something worse. It's as though you have a recording in your head that plays over and over again. That tape needs to be replaced with one that says the truth about who you are from God's perspective. Those are the things your child learned in the "Mirror, Mirror" section. You can help shape the way your son or daughter thinks about him or herself. Your young person looks to you as a mirror who will reflect God's truth about him or her. In this letter, if you have been harsh, critical, or have a negative pattern you think has affected your child, tell him or her you are sorry. Maybe your growing-up years were less than perfect; let your child know some of where you came from.

For example, my father loved me greatly. He sacrificed for me in many ways to help me have a head start in life, but my dad also was an alcoholic so his words often stung deeply. However, on a vacation with him one year, he told me his father had never said the words, "I love you" to him. That gave me new insight, compassion, and understanding of my father. You don't have to empty the closet of your past on these pages, but you might have a story, or a snapshot, of something from your growing-up years that would help your child see how God has changed you—or is changing you into His image.

Maybe you were fortunate to have a very godly heritage. Share stories of your parents, grandparents, and other relatives that will help reinforce the faith of your child.

Be a mirror to your children. Reflect to them one "You Are" from the "Mirror" section, or a Beatitude you think best captures your child this year.

As a father has compassion on his children,

so the Lord has compassion on those who fear him.

Psalm 103:13

REFLECTIONS cont'd

It's a Party!
Kid Celebrations of Faith

You are getting older now. You are probably beginning to wonder what life will really be like when you grow up. So many decisions are ahead: what will you study in high school and college—and where will you go to college? Whom will you marry? Where will you live? What will your career be? How will you serve God? Discerning the will of God can feel like tricky business, but there are a few key principles that will help.

Delight yourself in God: Psalm 37:4 says "Delight yourself in the Lord and he will give you the desires of your heart." An amazing thing happens as you spend time with God, daily reading His Word. His heart is revealed and you begin to obey Him, and as you do, your heart begins to reflect God's heart. So the things that are important to God become important to you also. Things that make God sad will make you sad and things that make God happy will make you happy. Because of transformation (Romans 12:2), your requests, the things you pray about, will more likely already be things to which God wants to say yes! That's why the verse can say when you delight yourself in God He will give you the desires of your heart.

Develop a network of advisers: Proverbs 11:14 says, "For lack of guidance a nation falls, but many advisers make victory sure." People make better decisions when they can talk them out with others who are older and wiser and have walked with God longer. Who are these people in your life? List five or six people you consider to be your spiritual advisers: (Often a Sunday School teacher, pastor or youth pastor, or student youth group leader are these kinds of people. Sometimes your parents' friends can also be good advisers if they too are walking with Jesus.) _____

_____

_____

_____

Discerning the best: God wants you to find His best for you. He has a plan for you that brings hope and provides a future. God's plan for you is formed out of His love for you. One way to learn to discern God's best plan is to ask some easy basic questions.

What do you love to do?

What do you think you do well?

What do people compliment you for?

When do you think or say: I wish that never happened in the world. I wish I could change that.

Write three times when you helped someone else and you felt really good about it.

1 _____

2 _____

3 _____

Talk to your parents; ask them to answer these questions:
What do you think are some of your child's strengths?

What are some unique things about your child? For example, are there unique opportunities he or she has had? Are there unique skills he or she has gained? Are there unique talents he or she has developed or are beginning to develop? Has there been anything unique about the place or way he or she has been raised? (As you talk to your parents, write down the uniquenesses they see in you.)

To equip us to do His will, God also gives each person spiritual gifts. These gifts have a special reason. Read this verse and see if you can figure out why God gives spiritual gifts:

"To prepare God's people for works of service, so that the body of Christ may be built up" (Eph. 4:12).

Why did God give us gifts?

Now read this passage and underline each different kind of gift.

Romans 12:4-8

Just as each of us has one body with many members, and these members do not all have the same function, so in Christ we who are many form one body, and each member belongs to all the others. We have different gifts, according to the grace given us. If a man's gift is prophesying let him use it in proportion to his faith. If it is serving, let him serve; if it is teaching, let him teach; if it is encouraging, let him encourage; if it is contributing to the needs of others, let him give generously; if it is leadership, let him govern diligently; if it is showing mercy, let him do it cheerfully.

Who chooses what gift you have? _____

Is one gift more important than another? _____

1 Corinthians 12:18

But in fact God has arranged the parts in the body, every one of them, just as he wanted them to be.

1 Corinthians 12:24-25

While our presentable parts need no special treatment. But God has combined the members of the body and has given greater honor to the parts that lacked it, so that there should be no division in the body, but that its parts should have equal concern for each other.

The best way to figure out your spiritual gift is to try lots of different things in ministry. Volunteer in many different ways at your church and in your community. On the next page is a list of spiritual gifts based on the Bible and some ways you might want to use them. Check three or four you'd like to try.

○ **THE BOSS:** Plan an activity, party, or event to tell people about Jesus or help people grow in their relationship with Jesus. (Gifts: Leadership/Administration. See 1 Cor. 12:5, 28; 1 Tim. 5:17; Rom. 12:8.)

○ **THE ARTIST:** Use your craftsmanship to create a project that is beautiful and that can be used at church or in your home to remind people about God. Ideas: banner, cross-stitch, wood project, painting. (Craftsmanship. See 2 Chron. 34:9-13; Acts 16:14; 18:3; Ex. 30:22-25.)

○ **THE MEGAPHONE:** Talk to someone about Jesus, share your story of faith, invite a friend to church, or show someone your *Celebrate!* scrapbook. (Evangelist. See 2 Tim. 4:5; Eph. 4:11; Rom. 10:15; Acts 5:42.)

○ **THE COUNSELOR:** Listen to a friend's problem and offer to pray with him or her. Try to find a Bible verse that will help your friend. (Exhortation/Wisdom. See 1 Cor. 2:1-3; 12:8; 2 Cor. 9:2; Rom. 12:8.)

○ **THE BANKER:** Give away money to help someone else. Give to a missionary, a needy family, a ministry, or your church. (Giving. See Mark 12:41-44; Rom. 12:8; Luke 18:12; 2 Cor. 8:1-7.)

○ **THE HELPER:** Help behind the scenes, set up chairs, pass out fliers, make punch, pick up after Sunday School or youth group. Do something a janitor or a secretary might do! (Helps/Serving. See 1 Cor. 12:28; Mark 2:3-4; 1 Tim. 6:2; Rom. 16:1-2; 1 Pet. 4:9-10; Rom. 12:7; Luke 22:22-27.)

○ **THE HOST OR HOSTESS:** Plan a party in your home, have someone spend the night and make him or her feel comfortable and share your best things during the stay, or make something and take it to a neighbor or an elderly person and stay and talk a few minutes. (Hospitality. See Acts 16:15; Rom. 12:9-13; Acts 21:16-17; Rom. 16:23.)

○ **THE PRAYER WARRIOR:** Pray for twenty minutes for one person who is really sick or hurting; pray out loud with someone who is sad; pray for your teachers on your way to or home from school. (Intercession. Col. 4:12; Acts 12:1-17; 1 Tim. 2:1-8; Acts 16:25-31.)

○ **THE BRAIN:** Offer to use your brain power to help another. Try tutoring, working in the sound booth or on a lighting crew or on computers for your church or another Christian organization. (Knowledge. See 1 Cor. 12:8; Rom. 15:14; 1 Cor. 13:8.)

○ **THE NURSE:** Help someone who is sick, disabled, or older or weaker than you are. Offer to work with special education children or younger children who need extra help in school. (Mercy. See Acts 9:36; Luke 10:33-35; Acts 16:33-34; Rom. 12:8.)

○ THE MUSICIAN: Play in a church band, orchestra, a solo at church, in a nursing home, or for youth group or children's church. You might try writing songs about God to play for people who don't go to church and then find a place to play them—at school, at a public event (a fair, music fest, for example). (Music. See 1 Chron. 16:41-42; 2 Chron. 5:12-13; 1 Sam. 16:16.)

○ THE TEACHER: If you know one thing about Jesus, you know one thing more than someone else. Teach someone younger than you something you know about Jesus. Gather up some kids from your neighborhood, or teach your younger brothers or sisters, or volunteer to help out in a younger classroom at church on Sunday or during the week. (Teacher. See 1 Cor. 12:28; Rom. 12:7; 1 Tim. 3:2; Eph. 4:11.)

○ THE WRITER: Write about Jesus and give it away. Create some greeting cards, write a short story or poem and give it to friends, or write a letter about an issue from a Christian point of view and send it to the editor of your local or school paper. (Writing. See Acts 15:19-20; Ps. 45:1; Phil. 3:1; 1 Tim. 3:14-15.)

Stuart Briscoe, author and pastor of Elmbrook Church, raised a family of children who are now grown and in ministry. Briscoe's motto: "Church isn't somewhere you go, it is something you are!"[1] And it seems studies back up his motto. Over 75 percent of the teens that feel alienated from religion indicated the church's failure to take them seriously and include them in significant roles is the major cause of their estrangement.[2] Use the church as a springboard for further service to God. Go on a family adventure and try to layer in a variety of ministry experiences into the lives of your children. Every person is a unique creation of God, and serving God is one of the surest ways for your child to grasp his or her uniqueness.

---

1. Jill Briscoe and Judy Golz, *I Caught a Little Big Fish* (Brookfield, WI: Briscoe Ministries, 1994) 59.
2. Ibid. 168.

KiD QUoTes!

"After church on a Sunday morning, a young boy suddenly announced to his mother, 'Mom, I've decided I'm going to be a minister when I grow up.'

"'That's okay with us,' the mother replied. 'But what made you decide to be a minister?'

"'Well,' the boy replied, 'I'll have to go to church on Sunday anyway, and I figure it will be more fun to stand up and yell than to sit still and listen.'"

MY QUoTes!

_____

_____

_____

_____

_____

_____

_____

_____

_____

3. J. Otis and Gail Ledbetter, *Family Fragrance* (Colorado Springs: Cook Communications Ministries, 1998) 45.

Happy Spiritual Birthday to You!

This is the final spiritual birthday celebration in this book. For this year's gift, give something that will encourage the child to record his or her own spiritual journey. Buy a blank journal, create a prayer diary or book of promises by writing your favorite verses at the top or bottom of each page in an empty journal. Buy a new Bible, one with large margin, and encourage the child to write and date when a verse speaks to his or her heart. Or buy another scrapbook and just keep going! Since your child either is a teen or will shortly be one, enlist him or her to create his or her own spiritual scrapbook. Buy an empty album, stickers, colorful paper, and markers and let him or her personalize the book and discover how he or she wants to record growth in the future. If your son or daughter has his or her heart set on going to a specific college, check to see if maybe the college bookstore has a binder or scrapbook or photo album that might be adapted, and challenge your adolescent to shift the focus from just recording what God has done, to dreaming about what God might do through him or her!

J. Otis and Gail Ledbetter of Heritage Builders ministry, give this creative idea:

"Start a journal to be shared exclusively with one or each of your children. Make an entry, telling your child a story, something about your past, what happened that day, or about a current subject. Place the book under her pillow. Now it is her turn to write something. When she is finished she can place it under your pillow. . . . There is no rush; it maybe exchanged every two or three days, once a week, or sporadically." [3]

Take a field trip to a Christian bookstore and buy the tools to navigate the future. Make sure your child has an exhaustive concordance, so he or she can find the verses on any word or topic in the Bible; a Bible dictionary and encyclopedia to locate background information and gain deeper understanding; a one or two-volume commentary will add clarity to the young person's own study as he or she reads what scholars in the field have recorded on various passages of Scripture. A book on how to study the Bible and one on apologetic issues like the reliability of the Bible, the deity of Christ, and so on will be helpful in answering their own questions and those of their friends. A good study Bible is the most important tool. Bibles come in all kinds of translations, paraphrases, for all levels of readers. They have options with all kinds of devotionals, guides, and study helps. Help your child have this goal: "Be diligent to present yourself approved to God as a workman who does not need to be ashamed, handling accurately the word of truth" (2 Tim 2:15, NASB).

Memory Makers
Advice from Parents Who've Been There

BIRTHDAY BOXES

Dave and Claudia Arp, in their book *Suddenly They're 13*, share an idea that you may want to adapt as your own children enter the teen years. "Becoming a teenager at our house was a big deal. After the family celebration, we planned another time to take our new teenager out to dinner with just the two of us. On this special occasion we tried to communicate the following message:

"'We are excited about your growing up. You are now a teenager, and we want to relate to you on a more adult level. In five short years you will be eighteen and will probably be leaving for college. We want you to be prepared to make your own decisions, run your own life, and function as an adult. So for the next five years on your birthday each year we will give you new and expanded privileges and responsibilities for the coming year. Our goal is that by the time you're eighteen you will achieve adult status—not only physically, but mentally, spiritually, and emotionally as well.'"[4]

The Arps then presented their teen with a small wooden box filled with 3 x 5 cards, and on each card was a new privilege or responsibility for the coming year in all areas including spiritual growth, and a variety of practical areas like relationships, finances, home responsibilities, school, and so on. (For more information on helping teens mature see *Suddenly They're 13* available through Marriage Alive.)[5]

You can adopt this birthday box tradition, and you may also adapt it to include a spiritual birthday box that is given in celebration of your teen's spiritual birthday at a different time of year from his or her physical birthday. The spiritual birthday box could be filled with the latest Christian videos, music CDs, computer games, teen magazines, books, and devotionals. It might seem expensive to give two gifts a year, one for a teen's natural birthday, and one for a spiritual celebration, but all in all, it is still less expensive than counseling, a run-in with juvenile authorities, or the emotional price you might pay later in life with an adult child who hasn't fully grown up.

---

4. David and Claudia Arp, *Suddenly They're 13 or the Art of Hugging a Cactus* (Grand Rapids, MI: Harper Collins, 1999) 67.
5. Ibid. 67.

Dennis and Barbara Rainey, leaders of Family Life Today Ministries, note, "Character development is a major theme of God's work in people. And it's one of the major assignments given us parents. Character is how your child responds to authority and life's circumstances." [6] For years now, you have been building character into your child, now compliment your child's character! Write an introduction for your child as if he or she is being asked to speak, perform, or is being highlighted or awarded for his or her uniqueness or strengths. Here's an example of one written for our thirteen-year-old son, Zach.

I'd like to introduce to you one of my favorite people. Zach Farrel is an amazing athlete. No matter the sport—skateboarding, football, baseball, basketball, snowboarding—he has always been a natural. But it isn't for his athletics, or even for his honor roll scholastics, he is being honored tonight. It isn't even for his awesome culinary skills, or his unique sense of humor that we honor him, although we all benefit from those traits. No, tonight he is being honored for his fantastic friendship skills. Zach is loyal, hardworking, and compassionate. He loves little children and will do whatever it takes to help others succeed. The Bible character that Zach comes closest to resembling is John the Baptist, who said of Jesus, "He must increase, but I must decrease" (John 3:30, KJV). Please welcome with me, the best friend you might ever have, my son, Zachery Farrel.

---

6. Dennis and Barbara Rainey with Bruce Nygren, *Parenting Today's Adolescent: Helping Your Child Avoid the Traps of the Preteen and Teen Years* (Nashville: Thomas Nelson, 1998) 38.

This is your opportunity to write a tangible blessing. Often, in early biblical times, fathers would prophesy, or proclaim, what they thought God would do with and for their children. Write a letter to God and express your hopes, dreams, fears, and feelings about the future in regard to your child. Or write a letter to your child lining out the next five to seven years, expressing your hopes and dreams for your son or daughter. Be sure to compliment the growth you have seen so far. You might choose a fond memory from childhood and compare it to a hope you have for your child in the future. Create a written letter that will carry your teen through the bumpy roads ahead and help land him or her securely on the shores of adulthood—which will be right around the corner!

Dear God

Write a letter to Jesus thanking Him for the growth you have seen in your life while you have been completing this scrapbook. Also, be sure and write to Him and express how you feel about moving into adulthood. Tell Him your hopes and dreams and any fears about the future. God's Word says, "There is no fear in love. But perfect love drives out fear" (1 John 4:18). Let God's perfect love take away any of your fears. First Peter 5:7 says to "cast all your anxiety on him because he cares for you." Express to God what you hope is His best for your life. Whom do you want to date, marry, how would you like to serve Him, what career would you like? In 1 Thessalonians 4:1 God encourages us to "excel still more" (NASB). List ways you need God's help to be all that you were designed to be. What are areas you'd like to improve on and you need God's help with? Ask Him for help. He loves you!

_____

_____

_____

_____

_____

_____

_____

We will not hide them from their children;

we will tell the next generation

the praiseworthy deeds of the Lord,

his power, and the wonders he has done.

Psalm 78:4

Speaking the truth in love, we will in all things grow up into him ..., Christ.
Ephesians 4:15

Crave pure spiritual milk, so that by it you may grow up in your salvation.
1 Peter 2:2

Become mature, attaining to the whole measure of the fullness of Christ.
Ephesians 4:13

That you may stand firm in all the will of God, mature and fully assured.
Colossians 4:12

*But solid food is for the mature, who by constant use have trained themselves
to distinguish good from evil.*
Hebrews 5:14

*But grow in the grace and knowledge of our Lord and Savior Jesus Christ. To
him be glory both now and forever! Amen.*
2 Peter 3:18

I Made a Big Decision!

I made a big decision. I prayed and asked Jesus into my life. I accepted Him as my Savior and Lord. Savior means that He saved or rescued me from bad. Lord means He's my leader. He's also my best friend.

The date I prayed and made my big decision was:

———

I'd heard the truths from God's Word, the Bible. Truth is fact, like:

1. God loves me. (John 3:16)
2. I am a sinner. That means I'm not perfect. Nobody is.

My sin can be seen in ugly words, bad thoughts, or disobedient actions. My sin separates me from friendship with God. (Rom. 3:23, 6:23)

3. Jesus is the way to God. Only Jesus is perfect. He died on the cross for my sins, for everyone's sins, then rose again, and went to heaven. He fixed my friendship with God. (John 1:12; Eph. 2:8-9)

The people who taught me these truths were:

———

Some people pray with those who tell them these things, like Mom or Dad, a pastor, a Sunday School teacher, or a friend. Sometimes a person likes to wait and pray to receive Jesus when he or she is all alone.

When I prayed to receive Jesus, I was:

_____

The place I prayed looked like:(draw a picture)

I was _____ years old when I made my big decision.

Now Jesus and I will be forever friends.

He promised He would never, ever leave me. Someday, I will live with Him in heaven, forever. (Heb. 13:5; John 14:1-3) Now, no matter how I feel, sad or happy, angry or upset, Jesus is always there.

I need to learn how to grow in my friendship with Jesus. Just like best friends, Jesus and I need to talk. He talks to me in the letter He wrote called the Bible. My Bible looks like: (Draw a picture.)

I talk to Jesus when I pray.

I don't have to use big or fancy words. I can talk to Him like a friend. When I prayed to receive Jesus the words I used were simple like:

_____

_____

I want to thank Jesus often for being my Savior, Lord, and best friend.

Another way I can grow in my friendship with Jesus is to obey His Word and serve Him by helping other people. This is the size of my helping hand. (Trace your hand.)

I can also go to church and hear and learn more from the Bible.

I go to _____church.

My pastor is _____.

My teachers are_____

_____

I can talk to my friends at church about the things I'm learning about God. That's called fellowship. My friends are:

_____

_____

_____

_____

I can also tell other people about Jesus and His love. Some people haven't made this big decision.
People I could tell are:

_____

_____

_____

_____

God promised to help me do all these things. God's Holy Spirit came into me when I asked Jesus to be my Lord. The Holy Spirit is God, but He doesn't have a body so He fits perfectly into my heart. The Bible tells me that the Holy Spirit will help me:

ⓖ Learn and understand. (John 16:13)

ⓖ Feel icky and sad when I sin. But I can confess my sin by saying I'm sorry to God. God forgives me and helps me to do right again. (1 John 1:9; John 16:8)

ⓖ Be brave and strong to do right. (2 Tim. 1:7; Acts 1:8)

This is what I look like now. Jesus makes me happy.
(Draw a picture of yourself.)

Resources for the Family

Family Life Today
Dennis Rainey
3900 N. Rodney Parham Rd.
Little Rock, AR 72212
1-800-FL-TODAY
www.familylife.com

Hearts at Home
900 W. College Ave.
Normal, IL 61761
309-888-MOMS
www.hearts-at-home.org

Heritage Builders
c/o Cook Communications
Ministries
4050 Lee Vance View
Colorado Springs, CO 80918
800-528-9489
www.heritagebuilders.com

Marriage Alive
David and Claudia Arp
888-690-6667
www.marriagealive.com

Masterful Living
Pam and Bill Farrel
629 S. Rancho Santa Fe #306
San Marcos, CA 92069
760-727-9122
Mliving@webcc.com
www.Masterfulliving.com

Moms in Touch
PO Box 1120
Poway, CA 92074-1120
800-949-MOMS

MOPS (Mothers of Preschoolers)
PO Box 102200
Denver, CO 80250-2200
303-733-5353
www.mops.org

Parent Talk/Family
Communications
PO Box 3700
Tucson, AZ 85740
800-776-1060
www.flc.org/parenttalk

Faith Parenting is an imprint of
Cook Communications Ministries, Colorado Springs, Colorado 80918
Cook Communications, Paris, Ontario
Kingsway Communications, Eastbourne, England

CELEBRATE! I MADE A BIG DECISION
© 2000 by Pam Farrel. All rights reserved.

Printed in Singapore.
1 2 3 4 5 6 7 8 9 10 Printing/Year 04 03 02 01 00

Unless otherwise noted, all Scripture references are from the *Holy Bible, New
International Version*®. Copyright © 1973, 1978, 1984 by International Bible
Society. Used by permission of Zondervan Publishing House. All rights
reserved. Other Scriptures are taken from the *International Children's Bible,
New Century Version*, copyright © 1986 by Sweet Publishing, Fort Worth, Texas
76137. Used by permission (NCV); the *King James Version* (KJV); *New American
Standard Version*, © The Lockman Foundation 1960, 1962, 1963, 1968, 1971,
1972, 1973, 1975, 1977 (NASB).

Editor: Lee Hough
Design: Image Studios

Boy: ISBN 0-78143-453-X
Girl: ISBN 0-78143-465-3